The Faith We Sing

Pew Edition

Abingdon Press
Nashville, Tennessee

INTRODUCTION

The denominational hymnals published during the past generation are now old enough to require major supplementation. Many new hymns, songs, and choruses have appeared. Experience has shown that some older treasures were missed when the current hymnals were compiled. Denominational hymnal supplements are being produced to include new music and old favorites.

The Faith We Sing has been compiled primarily as a supplement to *The United Methodist Hymnal* (1989). Nothing here duplicates what is already in that hymnal. But *The Faith We Sing* is an ecumenical rather than a denominational book. It can also serve as a supplement to other hymnals now in use.

This hymnal supplement is a joint project of The United Methodist Publishing House and The General Board of Discipleship of The United Methodist Church. It has been compiled by a joint committee consisting of Publishing House staff Bill Gnegy and Gary Alan Smith, Board of Discipleship staff Daniel Benedict and Anne Burnette Hook, and general editor Hoyt L. Hickman. They have been advised by an ecumenical panel of expert consultants, all of whom have worked on recent hymnals. The task force was further assisted by about 180 reader consultants, primarily United Methodists, from all parts of the United States. The help of all these persons was crucial in determining the shape and contents of this book, and it is gratefully acknowledged.

The music reflects a wide diversity of Christian worship styles: praise music, new hymns, gospel songs, world music, American ethnic music, Taizé chants, and service music. The arrangement of contents, however, is topical rather than stylistic and is adapted from the arrangement of *The United Methodist Hymnal*.

This book is the Pew Edition, designed for the congregation's use. Harmony is provided where music is designed to be sung by the congregation in parts. Only the melody line is provided where music is designed to be sung in unison. It is part of a larger package of printed resources that includes: (1) Singer's Edition for use by choirs, ensembles, or praise teams; (2) Accompaniment Edition for accompanists and instrumentalists; (3) Simplified Edition for home, small group, or church school use, or as an easy accompaniment edition; (4) Guitar Edition for lead and rhythm guitar players, pianists who play from "lead sheets," and worship leaders who lead from the guitar; (5) Worship Planner Edition with helps for the planner or planning team; and (6) Enlarged Edition, for worshipers who need larger pages, notes, and lyrics, and for music and song leaders who prefer larger print for leading congregational singing.

Four additional electronic resources are also available. They are: (1) CD-ROM Worship Planner Edition for those who use the PC to help plan worship; (2) MIDI Edition for those who use MIDI instruments in worship; (3) CD Audio Edition for those who want to play the MIDI recordings on their stereo equipment; and (4) Presentation Edition for worship leaders who use PowerPoint® files to project hymn lyrics during the service.

We live in a time when new music for worship is constantly appearing. Further resources for worship will continue to be developed. This book is a way station on the continuing journey of God's people.

Hoyt L. Hickman, General Editor

Pew Edition	ISBN 0-687-09054-7 (Cross and Flame)	Worship Planner Edition	ISBN 0-687-09056-3
Pew Edition	ISBN 0-687-04904-0 (Cross only)	Guitar Edition	ISBN 0-687-09059-8
Enlarged Edition	ISBN 0-687-04515-0	Compact Disc Accompaniment	ISBN 0-687-05216-5
Singer's Edition	ISBN 0-687-09055-5	CD-ROM Edition	ISBN 0-687-09217-5
Accompaniment Edition	ISBN 0-687-09058-X	MIDI Edition	Item No. 214822
Simplified Edition	ISBN 0-687-09057-1	Presentation Edition (lyrics projection)	ISBN 0-687-04523-1

06 07 08 09 — 20 19 18 17 16

Manufactured in the United States of America

We Sing to You, O God

2001

1. We sing to you, O God, the Rock who gave us
2. We wan-dered far from home out in a des - ert
3. You bear us through the world, an ea - gle to her
4. O God, e - ter - nal God, we hide with - in your

birth, let our re - joic - ing sing your name in
land, you shield - ed with your love our fear - ful
young, who ris - es on her wings and bears us
wings, the ev - er - last - ing arms to whom our

all the earth. To you, O God, let
pil - grim band. You kept us safe with -
toward the sun. We ride the vaults of
prais - es ring. Your word is true, your

songs be raised, in joy - ful hymns, our feast of praise.
in your arms and shel - tered us a - gainst the storm.
light and air and trust in your un - fail - ing care.
way is just, you are the God in whom we trust.

WORDS: Gracia Grindal (Deut. 32:11, 18; 33:27; Ps. 57:1; 66:2; 96:1-2)   DARWALL'S 148th
MUSIC: John Darwall; harm. from *Hymns Ancient and Modern*, 1875, alt.   66.66.88

2002 I Will Call upon the Lord

WORDS: Michael O'Shields (Ps. 18:1-2)
MUSIC: Michael O'Shields

I WILL CALL
Irregular with Refrain

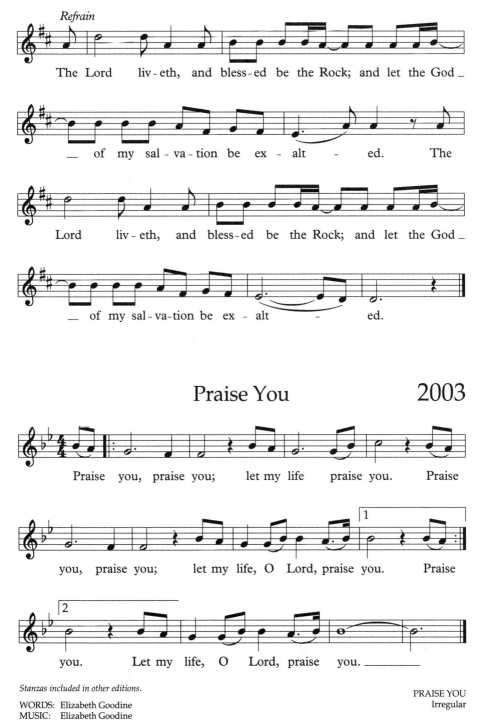

Refrain

The Lord liv-eth, and bless-ed be the Rock; and let the God _

_ of my sal-va-tion be ex-alt-ed. The

Lord liv-eth, and bless-ed be the Rock; and let the God _

_ of my sal-va-tion be ex-alt-ed.

Praise You   2003

Praise you, praise you; let my life praise you. Praise

you, praise you; let my life, O Lord, praise you. Praise

you. Let my life, O Lord, praise you. _____

Stanzas included in other editions.

WORDS: Elizabeth Goodine
MUSIC: Elizabeth Goodine

PRAISE YOU
Irregular

2004 Praise the Source of Faith and Learning

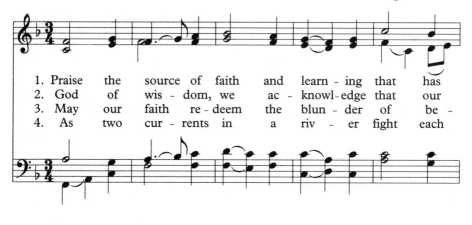

1. Praise the source of faith and learn-ing that has
2. God of wis-dom, we ac-knowl-edge that our
3. May our faith re-deem the blun-der of be -
4. As two cur-rents in a riv-er fight each

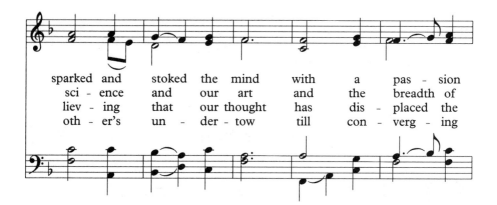

sparked and stoked the mind with a pas - sion
sci - ence and our art and the breadth of
liev - ing that our thought has dis - placed the
oth - er's un - der - tow till con - verg - ing

for dis - cern - ing how the world has been de-signed.
hu - man knowl-edge on - ly par - tial truth im - part.
grounds for won - der which the an - cient proph-ets taught.
they de - liv - er one co - her - ent stead - y flow,

WORDS: Thomas H. Troeger
MUSIC: Rowland H. Prichard; harm. from *The English Hymnal*

HYFRYDOL
87.87 D

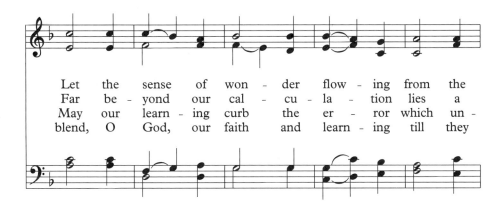

Let the sense of won - der flow - ing from the
Far be - yond our cal - cu - la - tion lies a
May our learn - ing curb the er - ror which un -
blend, O God, our faith and learn - ing till they

won - ders we sur - vey keep our faith for -
depth we can - not sound where your pur - pose
think - ing faith can breed lest we jus - ti -
carve a sin - gle course, till they join as

ev - er grow - ing and re - new our need to pray:
for cre - a - tion and the pulse of life are found.
fy some ter - ror with an an - ti - quat - ed creed.
one, re - turn - ing praise and thanks to you, their Source.

2005  Arise, Shine

WORDS: Gary Alan Smith (Isa. 60:1)
MUSIC: Gary Alan Smith

ARISE, SHINE
Irregular

Lord God, Almighty

1., 2. Lord God, Al-might-y, Sav-ior, Re-deem-er,
3. Fa-ther, we praise you. Je-sus, we love you.

on-ly true God to be wor-shiped and praised:)
Spir-it, we thank you for the gifts of new life:)

How can we tell you how much we love you?

Take now our lives, Lord, and teach us to love.

Stanzas included in other editions.

WORDS: Coni Huisman
MUSIC: Coni Huisman

COMFORT
Irregular

© 1984 Coni Huisman

Holy, Holy, Holy
(Santo, Santo, Santo)

Ho-ly, ho-ly, ho-ly. My heart, my heart a-dores you! My
¡San-to, san-to, san-to, mi co-ra-zón te a-do-ra! Mi

heart knows how to say to you: You are ho-ly, Lord!
co-ra-zón te sa-be de-cir: ¡San-to e-res, Dios!

WORDS: Argentine folk song (Isa. 6:3)
MUSIC: Argentine folk song

SANTO
Irregular

2008   Let All Things Now Living

1. Let all things now liv-ing a song of thanks-giv-ing to
2. The law God en-forc-es, the stars in their cours-es and

God the Cre-at-or tri-um-phant-ly raise, who
sun in its or-bit o-be-dient-ly shine; the

fash-ioned and made us, pro-tect-ed and stayed us, who
hills and the moun-tains, the riv-ers and foun-tains, the

guides us and leads to the end of our days. God's
deeps of the o-cean pro-claim the Di-vine. We,

ban-ners fly o'er us; God's light goes be-fore us, a
too, should be voic-ing our love and re-joic-ing; with

pil-lar of fire shin-ing forth in the night, till
glad ad-o-ra-tion a song let us raise, till

shad-ows have van-ished and dark-ness is ban-ished, as
all things now liv-ing u-nite in thanks-giv-ing: To

for-ward we trav-el from light in-to light.
God in the high-est ho-san-na and praise!

WORDS: Katherine K. Davis (Exod. 13:21; Ps. 148; 150:6)
MUSIC: Trad. Welsh melody
Words © 1938, 1966 E. C. Schirmer

THE ASH GROVE
6 6 11.6 6 11 D

O God Beyond All Praising

2009

1. O God be-yond all prais - ing, we wor-ship you to -
2. Then hear, O gra-cious Sav - ior, ac - cept the love we

day and sing the love a - maz - ing that
bring, that we who know your fa - vor may

songs can - not re - pay; for we can on - ly
serve you as our king; and whe - ther our to -

won - der at ev - ery gift you send, at
mor - rows be filled with good or ill, we'll

bless - ings with - out num - ber and mer - cies with - out
tri - umph through our sor - rows and rise to bless you

end: We lift our hearts be - fore you and
still: To mar - vel at your beau - ty and

wait up - on your Word, we hon - or and a -
glo - ry in your ways, and make a joy - ful

dore you, our great and might - y Lord.
du - ty our sac - ri - fice of praise.

WORDS: Michael Perry (Heb. 13:15)
MUSIC: Gustav T. Holst

THAXTED
13 13.13 13.13 13

2010   Praise Ye the Lord

Refrain

Praise ye the Lord,   Hal - le - lu - jah!

Ev - ery-bod - y praise the Lord. _

1. Praise God with the sound of the trum - pet,
2. Praise God with ho - ly cym - bals,
3. Praise God in the ho - ly tem - ple,
4. Praise God on top of the moun - tains,

praise God with the lute and the harp; ___
praise God with strings and with pipes; __
praise God for al - might - y deeds; __
praise God both day and night; __

praise God with tim - brel and danc - ing,
praise God with clash - ing cym - bals,
praise God for those boun - ti - ful mer - cies
praise God down in the low val - leys,

WORDS: J. Jefferson Cleveland (Ps. 150)
MUSIC: J. Jefferson Cleveland

NEW 150th
Irregular with Refrain

© 1981 J. Jefferson Cleveland

D.S. al Fine

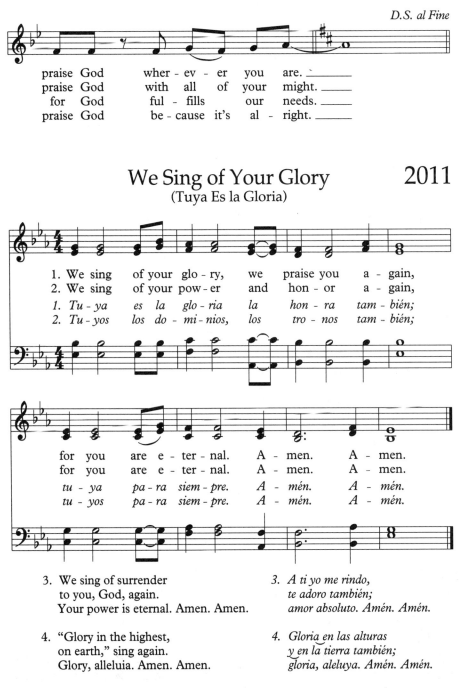

praise God wher-ev-er you are. _____
praise God with all of your might. _____
for God ful-fills our needs. _____
praise God be-cause it's al-right. _____

We Sing of Your Glory 2011
(Tuya Es la Gloria)

1. We sing of your glo-ry, we praise you a-gain,
2. We sing of your pow-er and hon-or a-gain,

1. Tu-ya es la glo-ria la hon-ra tam-bién;
2. Tu-yos los do-mi-nios, los tro-nos tam-bién;

for you are e-ter-nal. A-men. A-men.
for you are e-ter-nal. A-men. A-men.

tu-ya pa-ra siem-pre. A-mén. A-mén.
tu-yos pa-ra siem-pre. A-mén. A-mén.

3. We sing of surrender
to you, God, again.
Your power is eternal. Amen. Amen.

3. A ti yo me rindo,
te adoro también;
amor absoluto. Amén. Amén.

4. "Glory in the highest,
on earth," sing again.
Glory, alleluia. Amen. Amen.

4. Gloria en las alturas
y en la tierra también;
gloria, aleluya. Amén. Amén.

WORDS: Trad. Latin American; English trans. by S T Kimbrough, Jr. (Deut. 32:11, 18; RÍO DE LA PLATA
33:27; Ps. 57:1; 66:2; 96:1-2) 65.64
MUSIC: Trad. Latin American; harm. by Carlton R. Young

English trans. and harm. © 1996 General Board of Global Ministries, GBGMusik

2012 Let Us with a Joyful Mind

1. Let us with a joy - ful mind praise our
2. New - made earth was filled with light through God's
3. Daz - zling bright the sun o - beys God who
4. Stars and moon that span - gle night all de -
5. Crea - tures of the sea and land all are
6. There - fore with a joy - ful mind, praise our

Refrain

God for - ev - er kind,
all com - mand - ing might,
shines with bright - er rays, } rich with mer - cies that en -
pend on heav - en's light,
fed by God's own hand,
God for - ev - er kind,

dure, ev - er faith - ful, ev - er sure.

WORDS: John Milton, adapt. by Thomas H. Troeger (Ps. 136) INNOCENTS
MUSIC: From *The Parish Choir* (1850) 77.77

Bless the Lord

Bless the Lord my soul and bless God's ho - ly name.

Bless the Lord my soul who leads me in - to life.

WORDS: Jacques Berthier (Ps. 103:1)
MUSIC: Jacques Berthier and the Taizé Community

BLESS THE LORD (TAIZÉ)
Irregular

Alleluia

Al - le - lu - ia, al - le - lu - ia, al - le - lu - ia.

Al - le - lu - ia, al - le - lu - ia, al - le - lu - ia.

TAIZÉ ALLELUIA
Irregular

MUSIC: Jacques Berthier

2015 Bless His Holy Name

Bless the Lord, O my soul, and all that is with-
in me, bless his ho - ly name.
He has done great things, he has done great things,
he has done great things, bless his ho - ly name.

Fine

D.C. al Fine

WORDS: Andraé Crouch (Ps. 103:1)
MUSIC: Andraé Crouch
© 1973 Bud John Songs, Inc.

BLESS HIS HOLY NAME
Irregular

2016 Glorify Thy Name

1. Fa - ther,
2. Je - sus, } we love you, we wor - ship and a - dore you,
3. Spir - it,

glo - ri - fy thy name in all the earth. _____

WORDS: Donna Adkins (Ps. 86:12)
MUSIC: Donna Adkins
© 1976 Maranatha! Music, admin. by The Copyright Co.

GLORIFY THY NAME
Irregular

Glo - ri - fy thy name, glo - ri - fy thy name,

glo - ri - fy thy name in all the earth. _____

Come, Rejoice in God

2017

(Jubilate Servite)

Come, re - joice in God; praise him all the earth.
Ju - bi - la - te De - o om - nis ter - ra,

Serve your God, serve your God, glad - ly serve your God!
ser - vi - te Do - mi - no in lae - ti - ti - a,

Hal - le - lu - jah, hal - le - lu - jah, glad - ly serve your God;
Al - le - lu - ia, al - le - lu - ia, in lae - ti - ti - a!

hal - le - lu - jah, hal - le - lu - jah, glad - ly serve your God!
Al - le - lu - ia, al - le - lu - ia, in lae - ti - ti - a!

May be sung as a round.

WORDS: Jacques Berthier (Ps. 100)
MUSIC: Jacques Berthier

JUBILATE SERVITE
Irregular

2018 Honor and Praise

1. Righ-teous and ho-ly in all of your ways;
2. Fill-ing the tem-ple, the work of your grace;

we come be-fore you with hon-or and praise.

Here to a-dore you for all of our days,

we come be-fore you with hon-or and praise. ____

Lord of the heav-ens, how faith-ful you are.

Shine down up-on us,
Rise in our spir-its, } O bright Morn-ing Star. ____

Righ-teous and ho-ly in all of your ways;

we come be-fore you with hon-or and praise.

WORDS: Twila Paris (Rev. 22:16)
MUSIC: Twila Paris

HONOR AND PRAISE
Irregular

Holy
(Santo)

WORDS: Guillermo Cuéllar from *La Misa Popular Salvadoreña*;
        English trans. by Josué Alvarez and Debi Tyree (Isa. 6:3)
MUSIC: Guillermo Cuéllar from *La Misa Popular Salvadoreña*

CUÉLLAR
87.87 D 87.87 D

2020

Praise the Lord with the Sound of Trumpet

1. Praise the Lord with the sound of trum - pet,
2. Praise the Lord with the crash - ing cym - bal,

praise the Lord with the harp and lute, praise the Lord with the
praise the Lord with the pipe and string, praise the Lord with the

gen - tle - sound-ing flute. Praise the Lord in the
joy - ful songs you sing. Praise the Lord on a

field and for - est, praise the Lord in the cit - y square,
week-day morn - ing, praise the Lord on a Sun - day noon,

praise the Lord an - y - time and an - y - where.
praise the Lord by the light of sun or moon.

Praise the Lord in the wind and sun-shine, praise the Lord in the
Praise the Lord in the time of sor - row, praise the Lord in the

dark of night, praise the Lord in the rain or snow or
time of joy, praise the Lord ev - ery mo - ment; noth - ing

May be sung as a canon.

WORDS: Natalie Sleeth (Ps. 150)
MUSIC: Natalie Sleeth

PRAISE THE LORD
Irregular

in the morn - ing   light.   Praise the Lord in the
let your praise de - stroy.   Praise the Lord in the

deep - est val - ley, praise the Lord on the high - est   hill,
peace and   qui - et,   praise the Lord in your work or   play,

praise the Lord; nev-er let your voice be   still.
praise the Lord ev-ery-where in   ev - ery   way!

What a Mighty God We Serve   2021

1., 4. What a might - y   God   we serve, __   what a

might - y God we serve, __   what a might - y God we serve, __

__ what   a   might - y   God   we   serve! __

2. Let us sing and praise the Lord …
3. Let us shout and praise God's name …

WORDS: Trad. African folk song; adapt. by Jack Schrader
MUSIC: Trad. African folk song; adapt. by Jack Schrader
Adapt. © 1995 Hope Publishing Co.

MIGHTY GOD
Irregular

2022   Great Is the Lord

Refrain

Great is the Lord, he is ho-ly and just; by his pow-er we trust in his love. Great is the Lord, he is faith-ful and true; by his mer-cy he proves he is love.

1., 2. Great is the Lord and wor-thy of glo-ry! Great is the Lord and wor-thy of praise. Great is the Lord; now lift up your voice, now lift up your voice: Great _____ is the Lord! _____ Great _____ is the Lord!

3. Great are you, Lord, and wor-thy of glo-ry! Great are you, Lord, and wor-thy of praise. Great are you, Lord; I lift up my voice, I lift up my voice: Great _____ are you, Lord! _____ Great _____ are you, Lord!

First time D.C.
Second time D.S.

WORDS: Michael W. Smith and Deborah D. Smith (Ps. 35:27)
MUSIC: Michael W. Smith and Deborah D. Smith

GREAT IS THE LORD
Irregular with Refrain

How Majestic Is Your Name

WORDS: Michael W. Smith (Ps. 8:1, 9; Isa. 9:6)
MUSIC: Michael W. Smith

HOW MAJESTIC
Irregular

2024   From the Rising of the Sun

From the ris - ing of the sun ____ to the
go-ing down of the same, __ the name of the
Lord shall be praised. _____ From the
ris - ing of the sun __ to the go-ing down of the same, __
__ the name of the Lord shall be
praised. _____ So praise ye the
Lord. _____ Praise ye the
Lord. From the ris - ing of the sun __

WORDS: Anon. (Ps. 113:3)
MUSIC: Anon.

RISING SUN
Irregular

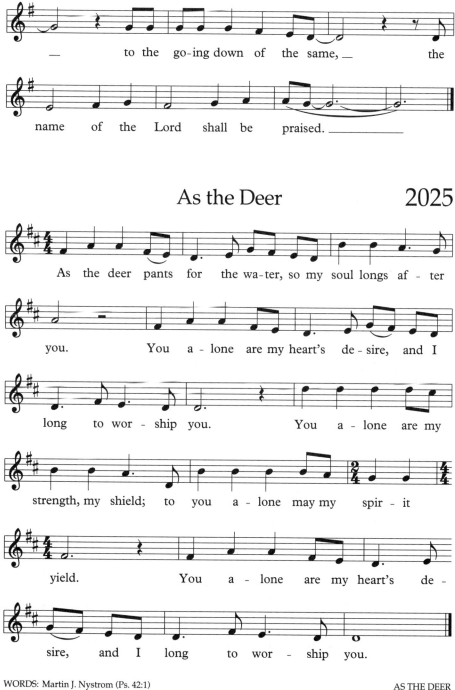

As the Deer

2025

WORDS: Martin J. Nystrom (Ps. 42:1)
MUSIC: Martin J. Nystrom

AS THE DEER
Irregular

2026   Halle, Halle, Halleluja

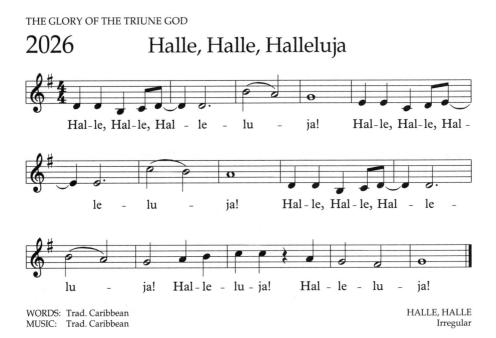

Hal-le, Hal-le, Hal - le - lu - ja! Hal-le, Hal-le, Hal -
le - lu - ja! Hal - le, Hal - le, Hal - le -
lu - ja! Hal-le-lu-ja! Hal - le - lu - ja!

WORDS: Trad. Caribbean
MUSIC: Trad. Caribbean

HALLE, HALLE
Irregular

2027   Now Praise the Hidden God of Love

1. Now praise the hid - den God of love, in whom we
2. Who chal-lenged us, when we were young, to storm the
3. Who bids us nev - er lose our zest, though age is

all must live and move, who shep - herds us at ev - 'ry
cit - a - dels of wrong; in care for oth - ers taught us
urg - ing us to rest, but proves to us that we have

stage, through youth, ma - tur - i - ty, and age:
how God's true com - mun - i - ty must grow:
still a work to do, a place to fill.

WORDS: Fred Pratt Green (Acts 17:23-28)
MUSIC: English folk melody

O WALY WALY
LM

Clap Your Hands

WORDS: Handt Hanson and Paul Murakami (Ps. 47:1)
MUSIC: Handt Hanson and Paul Murakami

© 1991 Changing Church Forum

CLAP YOUR HANDS
Irregular

2029   Praise to the Lord

1. Praise to the Lord, ____ all of you, _____ God's
2. There is none like our God ____ in the heavens __ or on

ser - vants. _____ Bless - ed be the name ____ of our
earth, ____ who lifts the poor from the dust, ____ seat-ing

God _____ now and ev - er. _____ From the ris - ing
them ____ with the might - y, _____ who stoops to

Refrain

of the sun _____ may the Lord be
raise the weak and low:

praised. Praise to the name of the Lord! ____

WORDS: Ron Klusmeier (Ps. 113)
MUSIC: Ron Klusmeier

© 1972 Ron Klusmeier

RICHARDSON-BURTON
Irregular with Refrain

2030   The First Song of Isaiah

Refrain

Sure - ly, it is God who saves me; I will

trust in him and not be a - fraid. For the

Stanzas included in other editions.

WORDS: From *The Book of Common Prayer*, Canticle 9 (Isa. 12:2-6)
MUSIC: Jack Noble White

© 1977 H. W. Grey Co. c/o Belwin-Mills Publishing Corp., admin. by Warner Brothers Publications

FIRST SONG
Irregular

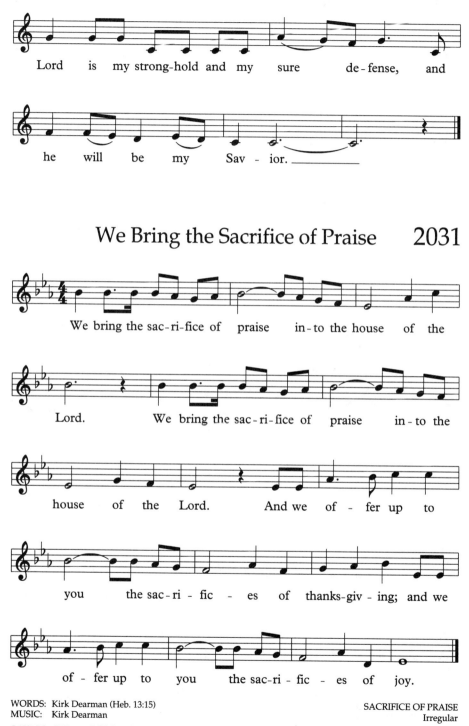

We Bring the Sacrifice of Praise   2031

Lord is my strong-hold and my sure de-fense, and he will be my Sav-ior. ___

We bring the sac-ri-fice of praise in-to the house of the Lord. We bring the sac-ri-fice of praise in-to the house of the Lord. And we of-fer up to you the sac-ri-fic-es of thanks-giv-ing; and we of-fer up to you the sac-ri-fic-es of joy.

WORDS: Kirk Dearman (Heb. 13:15)
MUSIC: Kirk Dearman

SACRIFICE OF PRAISE
Irregular

2032 My Life Is in You, Lord

My life is in you, Lord; my strength is in you, Lord; my hope is in you, Lord; in you, it's in you. My life is in you, Lord; my strength is in you, Lord; my hope is in you, Lord; in you, it's in you. I will praise you with all of my life, I will praise you with all of my strength; with all of my life, with all of my strength.

Second time to Coda

WORDS: Daniel Gardner
MUSIC: Daniel Gardner

MY LIFE
Irregular

D.S. al Coda

All of my hope is in you. _____ My

CODA

you, it's in you, in you. _____

Glory to God
(Gloria a Dios)

2033

1. Glo-ry to God, glo-ry to God, glo-ry in the high-est!
2. Glo-ry to God, glo-ry to God, glo-ry to Christ Je-sus!
3. Glo-ry to God, glo-ry to God, glo-ry to the Spir-it!

1. ¡Glo-ria a Dios, glo-ria a Dios, glo-ria en los cie-los!
2. ¡Glo-ria a Dios, glo-ria a Dios, glo-ria a Je-su-cris-to!
3. ¡Glo-ria a Dios, glo-ria a Dios, glo-ria al Es-pí-ri-tu!

To God be glo-ry for-ev-er! ⎫
To God be glo-ry for-ev-er! ⎬ Al-le-lu-ia, A-men!
To God be glo-ry for-ev-er! ⎭

¡A Dios la glo-ria por siem-pre! ⎫
¡A Dios la glo-ria por siem-pre! ⎬ *¡A-le-lu-ya, A-mén!*
¡A Dios la glo-ria por siem-pre! ⎭

Al-le-lu-ia, A-men! Al-le-lu-ia, A-men! _____

¡A-le-lu-ya, A-mén! ¡A-le-lu-ya, A-mén! _____

May be sung in call and response pattern.

WORDS: Trad. Peruvian (Luke 2:14)
MUSIC: Trad. Peruvian

MACHU-PICHU
Irregular

2034 Blessed Be the Name of the Lord

1., 4. Bless - ed be the name of the Lord, __

bless - ed be the name of the Lord, __

bless - ed be the name of the Lord __ most __ high. __

__

Bless-ed be the name of the Lord, __

__

bless-ed be the name of the Lord, __

Fourth time to Coda 1, 3

bless - ed be the name of the Lord __ most __ high. __

2

__ __ most __ high. __

The name of the Lord __ is __ a strong tow -

2. Glory to the name of the Lord ...
3. Holy is the name of the Lord ...

WORDS: Clinton Utterbach (Prov. 18:10)
MUSIC: Clinton Utterbach

UTTERBACH
Irregular

er, __ the righ-teous run in - to __ it __

1
__ and they are saved. __ The name of the Lord _

2
D.C. al Coda
__ and they __ are saved. __

CODA
__ most __ high. _____

Praise, Praise, Praise the Lord 2035

Praise, praise, praise the Lord.

Praise God's ho - ly name, Al - le - lu - ia.

Praise God's ho - ly name, Al - le - lu - ia.

Praise God's ho - ly name, Al - le - lu - ia.

WORDS: Trad. Cameroon
MUSIC: Trad. Cameroon
Words © 1994 Earthsongs

AFRICAN PROCESSIONAL
Irregular

2036 Give Thanks

Give thanks with a grate-ful heart, give thanks to the
Ho - ly One, give thanks be-cause he's
giv-en Je - sus Christ his Son. Give Son. And
now let the weak say, "I am strong"; let the
poor say, "I am rich be-cause of what the Lord has
done for us." And us." Give
us." Give thanks!

Last time to Coda

CODA

WORDS: Henry Smith (Luke 1:49-53)
MUSIC: Henry Smith

© 1978 Integrity's Hosanna! Music

GIVE THANKS
Irregular

I Sing Praises to Your Name 2037

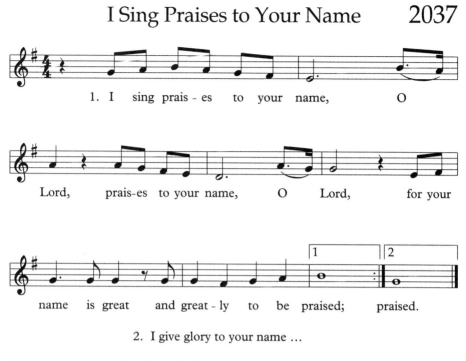

1. I sing prais - es to your name, O
Lord, prais-es to your name, O Lord, for your
name is great and great - ly to be praised; praised.

2. I give glory to your name ...

WORDS: Terry MacAlmon (Ps. 7:17; 9:2; 48:1; 96:4; 145:3)
MUSIC: Terry MacAlmon

I SING PRAISES
Irregular

© 1988 Integrity's Hosanna! Music

Father, I Adore You 2038

1. Fa - ther, I a - dore you, lay my life be -
fore you; how I love you.

2. Jesus, I adore you ...
3. Spirit, I adore you ...

May be sung as a canon.

WORDS: Terrye Coehlo (Matt. 6:9)
MUSIC: Terrye Coehlo

MARANATHA
66.4

© 1972 Maranatha! Music, admin. by The Copyright Co.

2039

Holy, Holy

1. Ho - ly, ho - ly, ho - ly, ho - ly,
2. Gra - cious Fa - ther, gra - cious Fa - ther,
3. Pre - cious Je - sus, pre - cious Je - sus,
4. Ho - ly Spir - it, Ho - ly Spir - it,
5. Hal - le - lu - jah, hal - le - lu - jah,

ho - ly, ho - ly, Lord God Al - might - y;
we're so blest to be your chil - dren, gra - cious Fa - ther;
we're so glad that you've re - deemed us, pre - cious Je - sus;
come and fill our hearts a - new, Ho - ly Spir - it;
hal - le - lu - jah, hal - le - lu - jah;

and we lift our hearts be - fore you as a to - ken of our love,

ho - ly ho - ly, ho - ly, ho - ly.
gra - cious Fa - ther, gra - cious Fa - ther.
pre - cious Je - sus, pre - cious Je - sus.
Ho - ly Spir - it, Ho - ly Spir - it.
hal - le - lu - jah, hal - le - lu - jah!

WORDS: Jimmy Owens
MUSIC: Jimmy Owens
© 1972 Bud John Songs, Inc.

HOLY HOLY
Irregular

2040

Awesome God

Our God is an awe - some God; he

reigns from heav - en a - bove with wis - dom,

WORDS: Rich Mullins (Deut. 10:17; Ps. 33:8; Matt. 13:54; Mark 6:2; Rev. 5:12; 19:6-7)
MUSIC: Rich Mullins
© 1988 BMG Songs, Inc.

AWESOME GOD
Irregular

Thou Art Worthy

2041

pow'r, and love. Our God is an awe-some God!

Thou art wor-thy, thou art wor-thy, thou art

wor-thy, O Lord, _____ to re-ceive glo-ry,

glo-ry and hon-or, glo-ry and hon-or and

power. _____ For thou hast cre-at-ed, hast

all things cre-at-ed; thou hast cre-at-ed all

things. _____ And for thy plea-sure they are cre-

at-ed; thou art wor-thy, O Lord. _____

WORDS: Pauline Michael Mills (Rev. 4:11)
MUSIC: Pauline Michael Mills

WORTHY
Irregular

© 1963, 1975, renewed 1991 Fred Bock Music Co., Inc.

2042 How Lovely, Lord, How Lovely

1. How love-ly, Lord, how love-ly is your a-bid-ing
2. In your blest courts to wor-ship, O God, a sin-gle
3. A sun and shield for-ev-er are you, O God most

place; my soul is long-ing, faint-ing, to
day is bet-ter than a thou-sand if
high; you show-er us with bless-ings no

feast up-on your grace. The spar-row finds a
I from you should stray. I'd rath-er keep the
good will you de-ny. The saints, your grace re-

shel-ter, a place to build her nest; and
en-trance and claim you as my Lord than
ceiv-ing, from strength to strength shall go, and

so your tem-ple calls us with-in its walls to rest.
rev-el in the rich-es the ways of sin af-ford.
from their life shall riv-ers of bless-ings o-ver-flow.

WORDS: Arlo Duba (Ps. 84)
MUSIC: Hal H. Hopson

MERLE'S TUNE
76.76 D

Words © 1986 Hope Publishing Co.; music © 1983 Hope Publishing Co.

2043 Alleluia

Al-le-lu-ia! Al-le-lu-ia!

Stanzas included in other editions.

MUSIC: Fintan O'Carroll and Christopher Walker

CELTIC ALLELUIA
Irregular

© 1985 Fintan O'Carroll and Christopher Walker, admin. by OCP Publications

My Gratitude Now Accept, O God 2044
(Gracias, Señor)

1. My grat-i-tude now ac-cept, O God, for ten-der
2. From all your boun-ty I give to you; for all the
1. Gra-cias, Se-ñor, por lo que me das, gra-cias por
2. Te doy de lo que tú me das, con go-zo

care that you pro-vide; for your a-bun-dant
bless-ings you im-part. Re-ceive this of-fer-
ben-de-cir me. Gra-cias por tu fi-
en mi co-ra-zón. Re-ci-be hoy mi o-

1-3

faith-ful-ness. End-less is your sup-ply. _____
ing I bring. Re-ceive my joy-ful heart. _____
de-li-dad y por tu pro-vi-sión. _____
fren-da, te la en-tre-go a ti. _____

4

gifts from the heart ac-cept. _____
de lo que tú nos das. _____

3. I bring to you all my love and praise.
I glorify and bless your name.
Let me adore you, Holy One,
with every breath I take.

4. All that is living belongs to you;
all that I am in your hands kept.
From the abundance of your hand,
gifts from the heart accept.

3. Te amo, Dios, doy gloria a ti,
tú eres digno de loor.
Te adoro con mi vida
y con lo que me das.

4. Todo te pertenece a ti,
mi vida y todo mi ser.
Con gratitud te damos
de lo que tú nos das.

WORDS: Rafael Montalvo; English trans. by Raquel Mora Martínez (Ps. 24:1)
MUSIC: Rafael Montalvo

OFRENDA
Irregular

2045   Sing a New Song to the Lord

1. Sing a new song to the Lord, he to whom won-ders be-
2. Now to the ends of the earth see his sal-va-tion is
3. Sing a new song and re-joice, pub-lish his prais-es a-
4. Join with the hills and the sea thun-ders of praise to pro-

long! Re-joice in his tri-umph and
shown! And still he re-mem-bers his
broad! Let voic-es in cho-rus, with
long! In judg-ment and jus-tice he

tell of his power — O sing to the
mer-cy and truth, un-chang-ing in
trum-pet and horn, re-sound for the
comes to the earth — O sing to the

Lord a new song!
love to his own.
joy of the Lord!
Lord a new song!

WORDS: Timothy Dudley-Smith (Ps. 98)
MUSIC: David G. Wilson

ONSLOW SQUARE
77.11 8

PRAISE AND THANKSGIVING, *see further:*

2067   Amen, We Praise Your Name, O God ("Amen Siakudumisa")
2274   Come, All You People ("Uyai Mose")
2084   Come, Let Us with Our Lord Arise
2276   Glory to God in the Highest (Haas)
2068   I Love You, Lord
2065   More Precious than Silver
2087   We Will Glorify the King of Kings
2063   You Are Worthy ("Eres Digno")

Womb of Life

1. Womb of life, and source of be - ing, home of
2. Word in flesh, our broth - er Je - sus, born to
3. Brood-ing Spir - it, move a - mong us; be our
4. Moth - er, Broth - er, Ho - ly Part - ner; Fa - ther,

ev - ery rest - less heart, in your arms the worlds a -
bring us sec - ond birth, you have come to stand be -
part-ner, be our friend. When our mem - ory fails, re -
Spir - it, On - ly Son: We would praise your name for -

wak - ened; you have loved us from the
side us, know - ing weak - ness, know - ing
mind us whose we are, what we in -
ev - er, One - in - three, and Three - in -

start. We, your chil - dren, gath - er 'round you, at the
earth. Priest who shares our hu - man strug - gles, Life of
tend. La - bor with us, aid the birth - ing of the
one. We would share your life, your pas - sion, share your

ta - ble you pre - pare. Shar-ing stor - ies, tears, and
Life, and Death of Death, Ris - en Christ, come stand a -
new world yet to be, free of ser - vant, lord, and
word of world made new, ev - er sing - ing, ev - er

laugh - ter, we are nur-tured by your care.
mong us, send the Spir - it by your breath.
mas - ter, free for love and u - ni - ty.
prais - ing, one with all, and one with you.

WORDS: Ruth Duck (John 1:14; 20:19-23)
MUSIC: Skinner Chávez-Melo

RAQUEL
87.87 D

2047   Bring Many Names

Descant, st. 6   Great, liv - ing God,

1. Bring man - y names,   beau - ti - ful and
2. Strong moth - er God,   work - ing night and
3. Warm fa - ther God,   hug - ging ev - ery
4. Old, ach - ing God,   grey with end - less
5. Young, grow - ing God,   ea - ger, on the
6. Great, liv - ing God,   nev - er ful - ly

nev - er ful - ly known, dark - ness far be - yond our

good,   cel - e - brate, in par - a - ble and
day,   plan - ning all the won - ders of cre -
child,   feel - ing all the strains of hu - man
care,   calm - ly pierc - ing e - vil's new dis -
move,   say - ing no to false - hood and un -
known,   joy - ful dark - ness far be - yond our

see - ing, clos - er yet than breath - ing

sto - ry, ho - li - ness in glo - ry,
a - tion, set - ting each e - qua - tion,
liv - ing, car - ing and for - giv - ing
guis - es, glad of good sur - pris - es,
kind - ness, cry - ing out for jus - tice,
see - ing, clos - er yet than breath - ing,

WORDS: Brian Wren
MUSIC: Carlton R. Young

WESTCHASE
9 10.11 9

2048

God Weeps

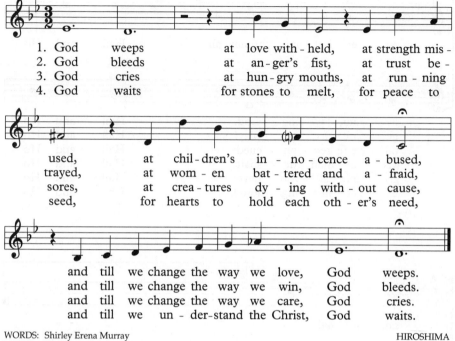

1. God weeps at love with-held, at strength mis-
2. God bleeds at an-ger's fist, at trust be-
3. God cries at hun-gry mouths, at run-ning
4. God waits for stones to melt, for peace to

used, at chil-dren's in-no-cence a-bused,
trayed, at wom-en bat-tered and a-fraid,
sores, at crea-tures dy-ing with-out cause,
seed, for hearts to hold each oth-er's need,

and till we change the way we love, God weeps.
and till we change the way we win, God bleeds.
and till we change the way we care, God cries.
and till we un-der-stand the Christ, God waits.

WORDS: Shirley Erena Murray
MUSIC: Carlton R. Young

HIROSHIMA
64.8 10

© 1996 Hope Publishing Co.

2049

God Is Here Today
(Dios Está Aquí)

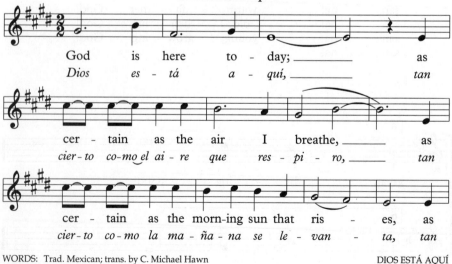

God is here to-day; _____ as
Dios es-tá a-quí, _____ tan

cer-tain as the air I breathe, _____ as
cier-to co-mo el ai-re que res-pi-ro, _____ tan

cer-tain as the morn-ing sun that ris-es, as
cier-to co-mo la ma-ña-na se le-van-ta, tan

WORDS: Trad. Mexican; trans. by C. Michael Hawn
MUSIC: Trad. Mexican; arr. by C. Michael Hawn and Arturo González

DIOS ESTÁ AQUÍ
Irregular

Trans. and arr. © 1999 Choristers Guild

cer - tain when I sing you'll hear my song. ____
cier - to co - mo que le can - to y me pue - de o - ír. ____

Mothering God, You Gave Me Birth 2050

1. Moth-er-ing God, you gave me birth in the bright
2. Moth-er-ing Christ, you took my form, of - fer - ing
3. Moth-er-ing Spir - it, nur - t'ring one, in arms of

morn - ing of this world. Cre - at - or, source of
me your food of light, grain of life, and
pa - tience hold me close, so that in faith I

ev - ery breath, you are my rain, my wind, my sun.
grape of love, your ver - y bod - y for my peace.
root and grow un - til I flow'r, un - til I know.

WORDS: Jean Janzen, based on the writings of Juliana of Norwich (15th cent.) MARYTON
MUSIC: H. Percy Smith LM

Words © 1991 Abingdon Press, admin. by The Copyright Co.

2051

I Was There to Hear
Your Borning Cry

1. "I was there to hear your born - ing cry, I'll be
3. "When you heard the won - der of the Word I was
5. "In the mid - dle ag - es of your life, not too
7. "I was there to hear your born - ing cry, I'll be

there when you are old. I re - joiced the day you
there to cheer you on; you were raised to praise the
old, no long - er young, I'll be there to guide you
there when you are old, I re - joiced the day you

Fine

were bap - tized, to see your life un - fold.
liv - ing Lord, to whom you now be - long.
through the night, com - plete what I've be - gun.
were bap - tized, to see your life un - fold."

2. I was there when you were but a child, with a
4. If you find some - one to share your time and you
6. When the eve - ning gent - ly clos - es in and you

faith to suit you well; in a blaze of light you
join your hearts as one, I'll be there to make your
shut your wea - ry eyes, I'll be there as I have

D.C.

wan - dered off to find where de - mons dwell.
vers - es rhyme from dusk till ris - ing sun.
al - ways been with just one more sur - prise.

WORDS: John Ylvisaker
MUSIC: John Ylvisaker

WATERLIFE
97.96 D

The Lone, Wild Bird

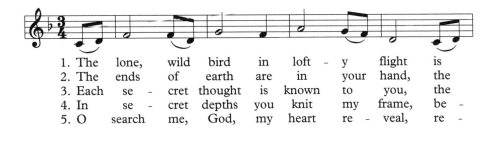

```
1. The   lone,   wild   bird   in   loft - y   flight   is
2. The   ends   of   earth   are   in   your   hand,   the
3. Each   se - cret thought   is   known   to   you,   the
4. In   se - cret depths   you   knit   my   frame,   be -
5. O   search   me,   God,   my   heart   re - veal,   re -
```

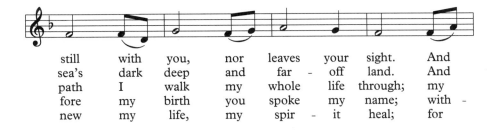

```
still   with   you,   nor   leaves   your   sight.   And
sea's   dark   deep   and   far - off   land.   And
path   I   walk   my   whole   life through;   my
fore   my   birth   you   spoke   my   name;   with -
new   my   life,   my   spir - it   heal;   for
```

```
I   am   yours!   I   rest   in   you,   Great
I   am   yours!   I   rest   in   you,   Great
days,   my   deeds,   my   hopes,   my   fears,   my
in   my   soul,   as   close   as   breath,   so
I   am   yours,   I   rest   in   you,   Great
```

```
Spir - it,   come,   rest   in   me,   too.
Spir - it,   come,   rest   in   me,   too.
deep - est   joys,   my   si - lent   tears.
near   to   me,   in   life,   in   death.
Spir - it,   come,   rest   in   me,   too.
```

WORDS: Sts. 1-3 by Henry Richard McFayden, alt.; sts. 4-5 by Marty Haugen (Ps. 139:2-4, 13-15, 23-24)

MUSIC: Walker's *Southern Harmony* (1835)

PROSPECT
LM

St. 4-5 © 1991 GIA Publications, Inc.

2053　　If It Had Not Been for the Lord

Refrain

If it had not been for the Lord on my side, tell me
where would I be, _____ where would I be. If it

1 *Fine*

2
be. 1. He kept my en-e-mies a-way; he let the
2. He nev-er left me all a-lone; he gave the

sun shine through a cloud-y day. He
peace and joy I'd nev-er known. He

rocked me in the cra-dle of his arm when he
an-swered when I knelt to real-ly pray, and in

D.S. al Fine

knew I had been bat-tered and scorned, so if it
vic-t'ry the Lord brought me his way, so if it

WORDS: Margaret P. Douroux
MUSIC: Margaret P. Douroux

WHERE WOULD I BE
Irregular with Refrain

© 1980 Margaret P. Douroux

2054　　Nothing Can Trouble
(Nada Te Turbe)

Noth-ing can trou-ble, noth-ing can fright-en.
Na - da te tur - be, na - da te es - pan - te.

WORDS: St. Teresa de Jesús; Taizé Community
MUSIC: Jacques Berthier

NADA TE TURBE
Irregular

© 1986, 1991 Les Presses de Taizé (France), admin. by GIA Publications, Inc.

Those who seek God shall nev-er go want-ing.
Quien a Dios tie - ne na-da le fal - ta.

God a - lone fills us.
So - lo Dios bas - ta.

You Are My Hiding Place 2055

You are my hid - ing place. You al - ways

fill my heart with songs of de - liv - er-ance, when-ev- er I am a -

fraid, I will trust in you, I will trust in

you. Let the weak say, "I am strong in the

Repeat ending | *Song ending*

strength of the Lord." Lord. I will trust in you."

May be sung as a canon.
WORDS: Michael Ledner (Ps. 32:7)
MUSIC: Michael Ledner

HIDING PLACE
Irregular

2056 God Is So Good

1. God is so good, God is so good,
2. God cares for me, God cares for me,
3. God loves me so, God loves me so,
4. God is so good, God is so good,

God is so good,
God cares for me,
God loves me so,
God is so good,
} God's so good to me.

WORDS: Trad.
MUSIC: Trad.

GOD IS SO GOOD
Irregular

2057 Be Still and Know That I Am God

Be still and know that I am God.

Be still and know that I am God.

May be sung as a canon.

WORDS: John Bell (Ps. 46)
MUSIC: John Bell

PSALM 46
Irregular

© 1989 WGRG The Iona Community (Scotland), admin. by GIA Publications, Inc.

2058 Shepherd Me, O God

Shep-herd me, O God, be-yond my wants, be-

yond my fears, from death in-to life. _____

Stanzas included in other editions.

WORDS: Marty Haugen (Ps. 23)
MUSIC: Marty Haugen

SHEPHERD ME
Irregular

© 1986 GIA Publications, Inc.

PROVIDENCE, *see further:*
2218 You Are Mine

I Am Your Mother

(Earth Prayer)

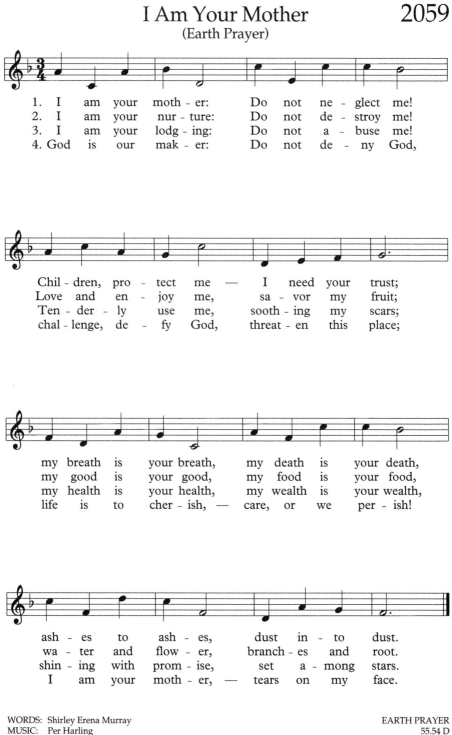

1. I am your moth-er: Do not ne-glect me!
2. I am your nur-ture: Do not de-stroy me!
3. I am your lodg-ing: Do not a-buse me!
4. God is our mak-er: Do not de-ny God,

Chil-dren, pro-tect me — I need your trust;
Love and en-joy me, sa-vor my fruit;
Ten-der-ly use me, sooth-ing my scars;
chal-lenge, de-fy God, threat-en this place;

my breath is your breath, my death is your death,
my good is your good, my food is your food,
my health is your health, my wealth is your wealth,
life is to cher-ish, — care, or we per-ish!

ash-es to ash-es, dust in-to dust.
wa-ter and flow-er, branch-es and root.
shin-ing with prom-ise, set a-mong stars.
I am your moth-er, — tears on my face.

WORDS: Shirley Erena Murray
MUSIC: Per Harling

EARTH PRAYER
55.54 D

2060 God the Sculptor of the Mountains

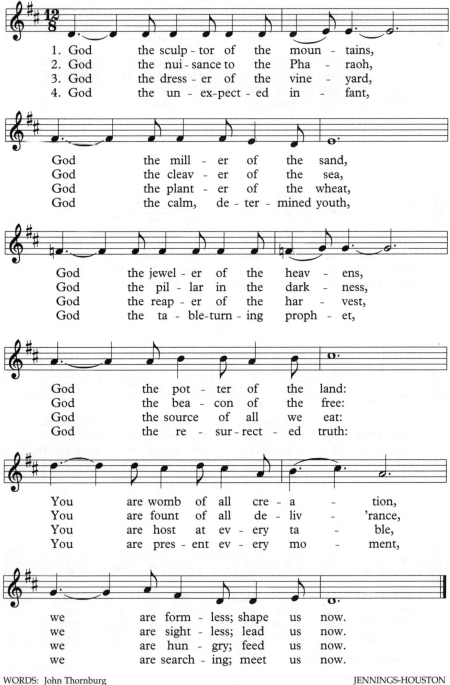

1. God the sculp-tor of the moun - tains,
2. God the nui-sance to the Pha - raoh,
3. God the dress-er of the vine - yard,
4. God the un-ex-pect-ed in - fant,

God the mill - er of the sand,
God the cleav - er of the sea,
God the plant - er of the wheat,
God the calm, de - ter - mined youth,

God the jewel - er of the heav - ens,
God the pil - lar in the dark - ness,
God the reap - er of the har - vest,
God the ta - ble-turn - ing proph - et,

God the pot - ter of the land:
God the bea - con of the free:
God the source of all we eat:
God the re - sur-rect - ed truth:

You are womb of all cre - a - tion,
You are fount of all de - liv - 'rance,
You are host at ev - ery ta - ble,
You are pres - ent ev - ery mo - ment,

we are form - less; shape us now.
we are sight - less; lead us now.
we are hun - gry; feed us now.
we are search - ing; meet us now.

WORDS: John Thornburg
MUSIC: Amanda Husberg

JENNINGS-HOUSTON
87.87.87

Praise Our God Above

(Harvest Song)

1. Praise our God a - bove, source of bound - less love: Spring wind, sum - mer rain, then the har - vest grain; pearl - y rice and corn, fra - grant au - tumn morn. Though our work is hard, God gives us re - ward.

2. God's care like a cloak wraps us hum - ble folk, makes all green things grow, rip - ens what we sow. Through God we are strong; sing our har - vest song. Sing praise, field and flower, praise God's might - y power.

WORDS: Tzu-chen Chao; trans. by Frank W. Price, alt. (Deut. 8:1-3, 6-10; Matt. 6:25-33)
MUSIC: Confucian Dacheng chant; arr. by W. H. Wong

HSUAN P'ING
55.55 D

CREATION, *see further:*

2041   Thou Art Worthy

2062 The Lily of the Valley

1. I have found a friend in Je - sus, he's ev - ery-thing to me,
2. He all my grief has tak - en, and all my sor-rows borne;
3. He will nev - er, nev - er leave me, nor yet for - sake me here,

he's the fair - est of ten thou-sand to my soul;
in temp - ta - tion he's my strong and might - y tower;
while I live by faith and do his bless - ed will;

the Lil - y of the Val - ley, in him a - lone I see
I have all for him for - sak - en, and all my i - dols torn
a wall of fire a - bout me, I've noth-ing now to fear,

all I need to cleanse and make me ful - ly whole.
from my heart, and now he keeps me by his power.
with his man - na he my hun - gry soul shall fill.

WORDS: Charles W. Fry (Deut. 31:6, 8; Ps. 36:8; Song of Sol. 2:1; 5:10; Hab. 2:4; Rom. 1:17; Rev. 2:17; 22:16)
MUSIC: William S. Hays; adapt. by Charles W. Fry

SALVATIONIST
Irregular

In   sor - row he's my com - fort,   in   trou - ble he's my   stay,
Though   all   the world for - sake me,   and   Sa - tan tempts me   sore,
Then   sweep - ing   up   to   glo - ry,   to   see his bless - ed   face,

he   tells me ev - ery care on him to   roll.
through   Je - sus   I shall safe - ly reach the   goal.
where   riv - ers of de - light shall ev - er   roll.

Hal - le - lu - jah!

He's the   Lil - y   of   the Val - ley,   the   bright and Morn - ing   Star,

he's the   fair - est   of   ten thou - sand to   my   soul.

2063 You Are Worthy
(Eres Digno)

You are wor - thy, ____ God al - might - y, _____ praise and
E - res dig - no, _____ e - res dig - no, _____ e - res

hon - or to you be - long. ____ You are long. ____
dig - no de a - do - ra - ción. ____ E - res ción. ____

_ King all glo - rious, __ all vic - to - rious, __ praise and
— Rey glo - rio - so, _____ ma - jes - tuo - so, _____ e - res

hon - or are yours a - lone. _____ King all lone. ____
dig - no de a - do - ra - ción. _____ Rey glo - ción. ____

WORDS: Trad. Latin American; English trans. by Raquel Mora Martínez (Rev. 4:11)   DIGNO
MUSIC: Trad. Latin American   LM

2064 O Lord, You're Beautiful

1., 3. O Lord, you're beau - ti - ful, your face is all I seek; and
2. O Lord, you're won - der - ful, your touch is all I need; and

when your eyes are on this child, your grace a - bounds to me.
when your hand is on this child, your heal - ing I re - ceive.

WORDS: Keith Green (Ps. 27:4, 8; Luke 5:12-13; Rom. 5:15)   BEAUTIFUL
MUSIC: Keith Green   SM

More Precious than Silver 2065

Lord, you are more pre-cious than sil - ver.

Lord, you are more cost - ly than gold.

Lord, you are more beau-ti-ful than dia-monds, and

noth-ing I de - sire com-pares with you. _____

WORDS: Lynn DeShazo (Ps. 16:2; 119:72; Prov. 3:13-15; 1 Pet. 2:7)
MUSIC: Lynn DeShazo
© 1980 Integrity's Hosanna! Music

DESHAZO
Irregular

Praise the Name of Jesus 2066

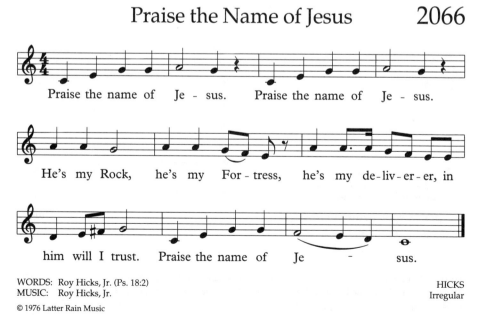

Praise the name of Je - sus. Praise the name of Je - sus.

He's my Rock, he's my For - tress, he's my de-liv-er-er, in

him will I trust. Praise the name of Je - sus.

WORDS: Roy Hicks, Jr. (Ps. 18:2)
MUSIC: Roy Hicks, Jr.
© 1976 Latter Rain Music

HICKS
Irregular

2067 Amen, We Praise Your Name, O God
(Amen Siakudumisa)

WORDS: Trad. Xhosa (South Africa); attr. to S. C. Molefe as taught by George Mxadana

MUSIC: Trad. Xhosa melody (South Africa); attr. to S. C. Molefe as taught by George Mxadana

MASITHI
Irregular

Sing a - men. _____
Ma - si - thi. _____

God.
sa.

A - men, ba - wo,
A - men, ba - wo,

praise your name, O God.
a - ku - du - mi - sa.

Ba - wo, ba -
Ba - wo, ba -

Sing a-men. _
Ma-si-thi. _

a-men, ba-wo,
a-men, ba-wo,

a-men, we praise your name, O God.
a-men si - a - ku - du - mi - sa.

wo,
wo,

ba-wo, ba-wo.
ba-wo, ba-wo.

We praise your name, O God.
Si - a - ku - du - mi - sa.

2068 I Love You, Lord

I love you, Lord, ___ and I lift my voice ___ to
wor - ship you, O my soul re - joice. Take
joy, my King, ___ in what you hear, ___ may it be a
sweet, sweet sound in your ear. ___

WORDS: Laurie Klein (Ps. 35:9)
MUSIC: Laurie Klein

I LOVE YOU, LORD
Irregular

2069 All Hail King Jesus

All hail King Je - sus! ___ All hail Em - man - u - el, ___
___ King of kings, Lord of lords, bright Morn - ing Star. ___
___ And through-out e - ter - ni - ty, I'll sing your prais - es; ___
___ and I'll reign with you through-out e - ter - ni - ty. ___

WORDS: Dave Moody (Matt. 1:23; 2 Tim. 2:12; Rev. 19:16; 22:16)
MUSIC: Dave Moody

KING JESUS
Irregular

He Is Exalted

He is ex-alt-ed, the King is ex-alt-ed on high; I will praise him. He is ex-alt-ed, for-ev-er ex-alt-ed and I will praise his name! __ He is the Lord, for-ev-er his truth shall reign; heav-en and earth re-joice in his ho-ly name. He is ex-alt-ed, the King is ex-alt-ed on high. _____

WORDS: Twila Paris (1 Chron. 29:11; Eph. 2:19-22)
MUSIC: Twila Paris

HE IS EXALTED
Irregular

© 1985 Straightway Music/Mountain Spring Music

Jesus, Name above All Names

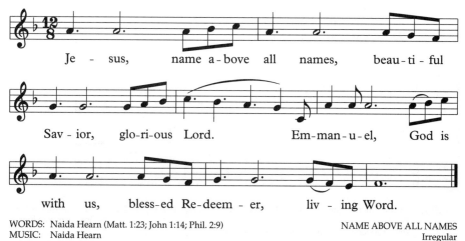

Je - sus, name a-bove all names, beau-ti-ful Sav-ior, glo-ri-ous Lord. Em-man-u-el, God is with us, bless-ed Re-deem - er, liv - ing Word.

WORDS: Naida Hearn (Matt. 1:23; John 1:14; Phil. 2:9)
MUSIC: Naida Hearn

NAME ABOVE ALL NAMES
Irregular

© 1974 Scripture in Song (a div. of Integrity Music, Inc.)

2072

Amen, Amen

WORDS: African American spiritual (Luke 2:7, 46-47; 5:1-3, 15; 1 Cor. 15:3-4; 1 Pet. 2:24; Rev. 22:5)

MUSIC: African American spiritual; arr. by Nelsie T. Johnson

Arr. © 1988 Nelsie T. Johnson

AMEN, AMEN
Irregular with Refrain

ly - ing in a man - ger ____ on
talk - ing to the el - ders; ____ how
preach - ing to the peo - ple, ____ —
bear - ing all my sins ____ in
rose on Eas - ter morn - ing, ____ and
Je - sus is my Sav - ior, ____ who

men, a -

Christ - mas morn - ing. ____
they all mar - veled! __
heal-ing all the sick ones! __
bit - ter ag - o - ny! ____
lives for - ev - er! ____
lives for - ev - er! ____

men, a - men, a -

2. See
3. See
4. See
5. Yes,
6. We're

men, a - men!

2073 Celebrate Love

Refrain 𝄋

Cel-e-brate love, love, love. _ Cel-e-brate love, love, love. _

_ Cel-e-brate love — so a-maz-ing. He's cre-at-

Fine

ing his won-der-ful love in you. _

1. We can cel - e - brate his love to - day.
2. We can sing a - bout his love for us.

Je - sus loves ev - ery - one. _ We can cel - e - brate new life _
Je - sus loves ev - ery - one. _ He is liv - ing here in - side _

D.S.

_ to - day. Je - sus loves ev - ery - one. _ }
_ of us. Je - sus loves ev - ery - one. _ } Cel - e - brate

WORDS: Handt Hanson
MUSIC: Handt Hanson

CELEBRATE LOVE
Irregular with Refrain

© 1991 Changing Church Forum

2074 Shout to the Lord

Shout to the Lord, all the earth, _ let us sing

pow - er and maj - es - ty, praise _ to the King.

Stanzas in other editions.

WORDS: Darlene Zschech (Ps. 47:1; 92:4; 96:1, 6, 10; 98:7-9; Isa. 49:13)
MUSIC: Darlene Zschech

ZSCHECH
Irregular

© 1993 Darlene Zschech/Hillsongs Publishing, admin. by Integrity's Hosanna! Music

Moun-tains bow down and the seas ___ will roar at the

sound of your name. I sing for joy at the work ___

___ of your hands, for - ev-er I'll love you, for-ev - er I'll stand.

Noth-ing com-pares to the prom - ise I have in you.

King of Kings 2075

King of kings and Lord of lords, glo - ry, hal - le - lu-jah!

King of kings and Lord of lords, glo - ry, hal - le - lu-jah!

② (opt. harmony)

Je - sus, Prince of Peace, glo - ry, hal - le - lu-jah!

Je - sus, Prince of Peace, glo - ry, hal - le - lu-jah!

May be sung as a canon.

WORDS: Sophie Conty and Naomi Batya (Isa. 9:6; Rev. 17:14)
MUSIC: Anon.

KING OF KINGS
Irregular

2076   O Blessed Spring

1. O bless - ed spring, _____ where Word and sign _____
2. Through sum - mer heat _____ and youth - ful years, _____
3. When au - tumn cools _____ and youth is cold, _____
4. As win - ter comes, _____ as win - ters must, _____
5. Christ, ho - ly Vine, _____ Christ, liv - ing Tree, _____

_ em - brace us in - to Christ the Vine:
_ un - cer - tain faith, _____ re - bel - lious tears, _____
_ when limbs their heav - y har - vest hold, _____
_ we breathe our last, _____ re - turn to dust; _____
_ be praised for this _____ blest mys - ter - y: _____

_ here Christ en - joins _____ each one to be _____
_ sus - tained by Christ's _____ in - fus - ing rain, _____
_ then through us warm, _____ the Christ will move _____
_ still held in Christ, _____ our souls take wing _____
_ that Word and wa - ter thus re - vive _____

WORDS: Susan Palo Cherwien (John 15:5; Rev. 22:14)
MUSIC: Trad. English melody; adapt. by Hal H. Hopson

GIFT OF LOVE
LM

Words © 1993 Susan Palo Cherwien, admin. by Augsburg Fortress; music © 1972 Hope Publishing Co.

— a branch of this _____ life - giv - ing Tree.
— the boughs will shout _____ for joy a - gain.
— with gifts of beau - ty, wis - dom, love.
— and trust the prom - ise of the spring.
— and join us to _____ your Tree of Life.

You Alone Are Holy 2077
(Sólo Tú Eres Santo)

1. You a - lone are ho - ly; _____ you a - lone are wor - thy; ___
2. You a - lone are ho - ly; _____ you a - lone are wor - thy; ___
1. Só - lo tú e - res san - to, _____ só - lo tú e - res dig - no, ___
2. Só - lo tú e - res san - to, _____ só - lo tú e - res dig - no, ___

— you are filled with splen - dor ____ and with awe - some won - der. _
— you are filled with splen - dor ____ and with awe - some won - der. _
— tú e - res her - mo - so _____ y ma - ra - vi - llo - so. __
— tú e - res her - mo - so _____ y ma - ra - vi - llo - so. __

— For our sins you suf - fered, _ died and res - ur - rect - ed, __
— Send your Ho - ly Spir - it; _____ may it shine up - on us. __
— En la cruz mo - ris - te _____ y re - su - ci - tas - te; __
— De - rra - ma tu Es - pí - ri - tu _____ y que tu luz bri - lle; __

— grant - ing us sal - va - tion, _ giv - ing us e - ter - nal life. __
— Let your won - drous glo - ry ____ with its ra - diance fill this place. _
— tú me dis - te vi - da ____ y muy pron - to vol - ve - rás. __
— que tu glo - ria lle - ne ____ aho - ra mis - mo es - te lu - gar. __

WORDS: St. 1 anon.; adapt. by Kenneth R. Hanna; st. 2 by Jorge Lockward;
English trans. by Raquel Mora Martínez (Rev. 4:11)
MUSIC: Anon.

QUERÉTARO
12 12.12 13

St. 2 © 1996, trans. © 2000 Abingdon Press, admin. by The Copyright Co.

2078   Alleluia

Al-le-lu -ia. Al-le-lu - ia. Al-le - lu -ia. Al-le-lu - ia. Al-le-lu - ia. Al - le-lu - ia. Now the Lord is ris'n in-deed. __
El Se - ñor re - su - ci - tó. ____

Stanzas included in other editions.

WORDS: Trad. Honduran
MUSIC: Trad. Honduran

HONDURAS ALLELUIA
Irregular

2079   Jesus Be Praised

Je - sus, we wor - ship you; with our voic - es filled with prais - es, Je - sus, we wor - ship you; songs of love we raise. Je - sus, Je - sus be praised! __ Je - sus, Je - sus be praised!

WORDS: Handt Hanson
MUSIC: Handt Hanson

JESUS BE PRAISED
Irregular

© 1996 Changing Church Forum

All I Need Is You

2080

1. — All I need is you, Je-sus,
2. — All I want is you, Je-sus,
3. My on - ly hope is you, Lord, my

all I need is you. You are the source of
all I want is you. You are the source of
on - ly hope is you. You are the source of

all I need. ___ All I need is you.
all I need. ___ All I want is you.
all I need. My on - ly hope is you.

WORDS: Dan Adler
MUSIC: Dan Adler
ADLER
Irregular

© 1989 Heart of the City Music

Thank You, Jesus
(Tino Tenda, Jesu)

2081

Thank you, Je-sus, a-men! Thank you, Je-sus, a-men! Thank you,
Ti - no ten-da, Je - su! Ti - no ten-da, Je - su! Ti - no

Je - sus, a - men! Al - le - lu - ia! A - men!
ten - da, Je - su! Ha - le - lu - jah! A - men!

WORDS: Trad. Shona; trans. by Patrick Matsikenyiri (Ps. 118:21; Rev. 11:17; 19:4)
MUSIC: African folk song; transcribed by Patrick Matsikenyiri
TINO TENDA
Irregular

© 1996 General Board of Global Ministries, GBGMusik

2082 Woke Up This Morning

WORDS: African American spiritual
MUSIC: African American spiritual; arr. by J. Jefferson Cleveland and Verolga Nix

WOKE UP THIS MORNING
Irregular

woke up this morn - ing with my mind, and it was stayed, Hal-le - lu, Hal-le -

Stayed on Je - sus, Hal-le - lu,

lu, Hal-le - lu - jah.

Hal-le - lu, Hal-le - lu - jah.

2. Oh, you can't hate your neighbor in your mind, if you keep it stayed, …
3. Makes you love everybody with your mind, when you keep it stayed, …
4. Oh, the devil can't catch you in your mind, if you keep it stayed, …
5. Oh, yes, Jesus is the captain in your mind, when you keep it stayed, …

2083 My Song Is Love Unknown

1. My song is love un-known, my Sav-ior's love to
2. God left the rich-est throne sal - va - tion to be -
3. Some-times they threw down palms and sweet-est prais - es
4. What has my Sov-ereign done? What makes this rage and
5. I sing my plain be - lief, one song my heart out -

me, love to the love - less shown, that
stow; but Christ as flesh and bone the
sang. Ho - san - nas and glad psalms through
spite? Christ gave new strength to run, re -
pours: nev - er was pain nor grief, nev -

they might love - ly be. O who am I, that
world re - fused to know. But, O my Friend, my
streets and mar - kets rang. Then "Cru - ci - fy!" is
stored the gift of sight. Sweet in - ju - ries! Yet
er was love like yours. This is my Friend, in

for my sake my God should take frail
Friend in - deed, who at my need did
all their breath, for blood and death they
they at these them - selves dis - please, and
whose sweet praise I all my days could

WORDS: Samuel Crossman (2 Cor. 5:15-19; Heb. 5:7-10)
MUSIC: John D. Edwards

RHOSYMEDRE
66.66.888

flesh and die? My God should take frail flesh and die?
life ex-pend; who at my need did life ex - pend.
thirst and cry; for blood and death they thirst and cry.
'gainst Christ rise; them-selves dis - please, and 'gainst Christ rise.
glad - ly spend; I all my days could glad - ly spend.

Come, Let Us with Our Lord Arise 2084

1. Come, let us with our Lord a - rise, our
2. This is the day the Lord has made, that
3. Then let us ren - der him his own, with

Lord, who made both earth and skies: who died to save the
all may see his love dis-played, may feel his res - ur -
sol - emn prayer ap-proach his throne, with meek - ness hear the

world he made, and rose tri - um - phant from the dead;
rec - tion's power, and rise a - gain, to fall no more,
gos - pel word, with thanks his dy - ing love re-cord,

he rose, the Prince of life and peace,
in per - fect righ - teous - ness re - newed,
our joy - ful hearts and voic - es raise,

and stamped the day for - ev - er his.
and filled with all the life of God.
and fill his courts with songs of praise.

WORDS: Charles Wesley (Ps. 118:24; 1 Cor. 6:14; Heb. 4:16)
MUSIC: Trad. English melody

SUSSEX CAROL
88.88.88

2085 He Came Down

He came down that we may have {love; peace; joy;} he came down that we may have {love; peace; joy;} he came down that we may have {love, peace, joy;} Hal-le-lu-jah for-ev-er-more.

Leader: Why did he come?

WORDS: Trad. Cameroon
MUSIC: Trad. Cameroon; transcribed and arr. by John Bell

HE CAME DOWN
Irregular

2086 Open Our Eyes

O-pen our eyes, Lord, _____ we want to see Je -

WORDS: Bob Cull (John 12:21; Eph. 1:17-18)
MUSIC: Bob Cull

OPEN OUR EYES
Irregular

sus, _____ to reach out and touch him, _____ and

say that we love him. _____ O-pen our ears, Lord, _

_ and help us to lis - ten. _____ O-pen our

eyes, Lord, _____ we want to see Je - sus. _____

We Will Glorify the King of Kings   2087

1. We will glo - ri - fy the King of kings, we will
2. Lord Je - ho - vah reigns in maj - es - ty, we will
3. He is Lord of heav - en, Lord of earth, he is
4. Hal - le - lu - jah to the King of kings, hal - le -

glo - ri - fy the Lamb; we will glo - ri - fy the
bow be - fore his throne; we will wor-ship him in
Lord of all who live; he is Lord a - bove the
lu - jah to the Lamb; hal - le - lu - jah to the

Lord of lords, who is the great I AM.
righ-teous-ness, we will wor-ship him a - lone.
u - ni - verse, all praise to him we give.
Lord of lords, who is the great I AM.

WORDS: Twila Paris (Ps. 93:1; Rev. 17:14)
MUSIC: Twila Paris

WE WILL GLORIFY
97.96

2088 Lord, I Lift Your Name on High

Lord, I lift your name on high;

Lord, I love to sing your prais - es.

I'm so glad you're in my life;

I'm so glad you came to save us.

You came from heav - en to earth _ to show the way, _

_ from the earth _____ to the cross _ my debt to pay; _

_ from the cross to the grave, _ from the grave to the sky; _

_ Lord, I lift your name on high.

WORDS: Rick Founds (1 Cor. 15:3-4)
MUSIC: Rick Founds

LIFT YOUR NAME ON HIGH
Irregular

IN PRAISE OF CHRIST, *see further:*

Wild and Lone the Prophet's Voice 2089

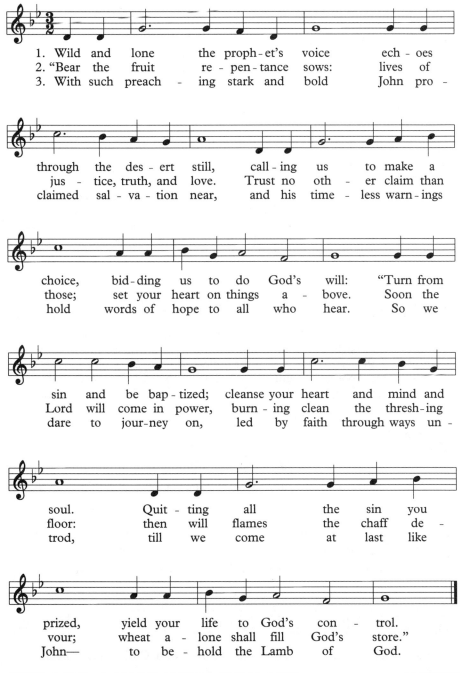

1. Wild and lone the proph-et's voice ech-oes
2. "Bear the fruit re-pen-tance sows: lives of
3. With such preach - ing stark and bold John pro -

through the des-ert still, call-ing us to make a
jus - tice, truth, and love. Trust no oth - er claim than
claimed sal - va - tion near, and his time - less warn-ings

choice, bid-ding us to do God's will: "Turn from
those; set your heart on things a - bove. Soon the
hold words of hope to all who hear. So we

sin and be bap - tized; cleanse your heart and mind and
Lord will come in power, burn - ing clean the thresh-ing
dare to jour-ney on, led by faith through ways un -

soul. Quit - ting all the sin you
floor: then will flames the chaff de -
trod, till we come at last like

prized, yield your life to God's con - trol.
vour; wheat a - lone shall fill God's store."
John— to be - hold the Lamb of God.

WORDS: Carl P. Daw, Jr. (Matt. 3; Mark 1:1-11; Luke 3:1-22; John 1:19-37)   LA GRANGE
MUSIC: David Ashley White   77.77 D

Words © 1989 Hope Publishing Co.; music © 1996 Selah Publishing Co.

2090

Advent Song
(Light the Advent Candle)

1. Light the Ad - vent can - dle, one: Now the
2. Light the Ad - vent can - dle, two: Think of
3. Light the Ad - vent can - dle, three: Think of
4. Light the Ad - vent can - dle, four: Think of
5. Light the Christ - mas can - dles, now: Sing of

wait - ing has be - gun; we have start - ed
hum - ble shep - herds, who filled with won - der
heaven - ly har - mo - ny; an - gels sing - ing
joy for - ev - er - more; Christ Child in a
don - key, sheep, and cow; birth - day can - dles

on our way, time to think of Christ - mas day.
at the sight of the child of Christ - mas night.
"Peace on earth" at the bless - ed Sav - ior's birth.
sta - ble born, gift of love that Christ - mas morn.
for the King, let the al - le - lu - ias ring.

Refrain

Can - dle, can - dle, burn - ing bright, shin - ing

in the cold win - ter night; can - dle, can - dle,

burn - ing bright, fill our hearts with Christ - mas light.

WORDS: Mary Lu Walker (Luke 2:1-20)
MUSIC: Mary Lu Walker

ADVENT CANDLE SONG
77.77 with Refrain

© 1975 Mary Lu Walker

The King of Glory Comes 2091

Refrain

The King of glo-ry comes, the na-tion re-joic-es.

Fine

O-pen the gates be-fore him, lift up your voic-es.

1. Who is the King of glo-ry; how shall we call him?
2. In all of Gal-i-lee, in cit-y or vil-lage,
3. Sing then of Da-vid's son, our Sav-ior and broth-er;

D.C.

He is Em-man-u-el, the prom-ised of a-ges.
he goes a-mong his peo-ple cur-ing their ill-ness.
in all of Gal-i-lee was nev-er an-oth-er.

WORDS: Rev. Willard F. Jabusch (Ps. 24:7-10; Matt. 1:23)
MUSIC: Trad. Israeli folk song
Words © 1966, 1982 Willard F. Jabusch, admin. by OCP Publications

KING OF GLORY
12 12 with Refrain

Like a Child 2092

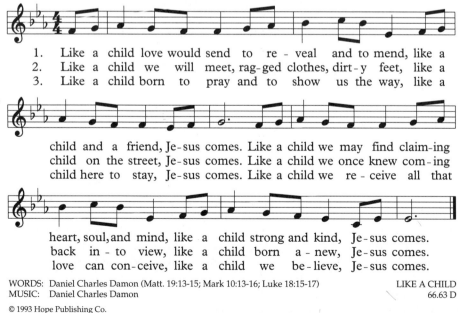

1. Like a child love would send to re-veal and to mend, like a
2. Like a child we will meet, rag-ged clothes, dirt-y feet, like a
3. Like a child born to pray and to show us the way, like a

child and a friend, Je-sus comes. Like a child we may find claim-ing
child on the street, Je-sus comes. Like a child we once knew com-ing
child here to stay, Je-sus comes. Like a child we re-ceive all that

heart, soul, and mind, like a child strong and kind, Je-sus comes.
back in-to view, like a child born a-new, Je-sus comes.
love can con-ceive, like a child we be-lieve, Je-sus comes.

WORDS: Daniel Charles Damon (Matt. 19:13-15; Mark 10:13-16; Luke 18:15-17)
MUSIC: Daniel Charles Damon
© 1993 Hope Publishing Co.

LIKE A CHILD
66.63 D

2093   The Snow Lay on the Ground

1. The snow lay on the ground, the stars shone bright, when
2. 'Twas Ma - ry, daugh-ter pure of ho - ly Anne, that
3. And thus that man - ger poor be-came a throne; for

Christ our Lord was born on Christ - mas night. Ve -
brought in - to this world the God made man. She
he whom Ma - ry bore was God the Son. O

ni - te a - do - re - mus Do - mi - num.* Ve - ni - te a - do -
laid him in a stall at Beth - le - hem; the ass and ox - en
come, then, let us join the heaven-ly host; to praise the Fa - ther,

Refrain

re - mus Do - mi - num.
shared the roof with them. Ve - ni - te a - do - re - mus
Son, and Ho - ly Ghost.

Do - mi - num. Ve - ni - te a - do - re - mus Do - mi - num.

*Venite adoremus Dominum = Veh-nee-teh ah-doe-reh-moos Doe-mee-noom

WORDS: Anglo-English carol (Luke 2:1-20)
MUSIC: English melody; adapt. by Charles Winfred Douglas

VENITE ADOREMUS
10 10.10 10 with Refrain

2094   Carol of the Epiphany

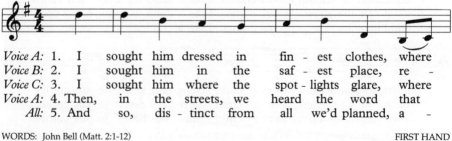

Voice A: 1. I sought him dressed in fin - est clothes, where
Voice B: 2. I sought him in the saf - est place, re -
Voice C: 3. I sought him where the spot - lights glare, where
Voice A: 4. Then, in the streets, we heard the word that
All: 5. And so, dis - tinct from all we'd planned, a -

WORDS: John Bell (Matt. 2:1-12)
MUSIC: John Bell

FIRST HAND
LM

mon - ey talks and stat - us grows; but power and wealth he
mote from crime or cheap dis - grace; but safe - ty nev - er
crowds col - lect and crit - ics stare; but no one knew his
seemed, for all the world, ab - surd: That those who could no
mong the poor - est of the land, we did what few might

nev - er chose: It seemed he lived in pov - er - ty.
knew his face: It seemed he lived in jeop - ar - dy.
pres - ence there: It seemed he lived in ob - scu - ri - ty.
gifts af - ford were en - ter - tain - ing Christ the Lord.
un - der - stand: We touched God in a ba - by's hand.

Star-Child 2095

1. Star - Child, earth - Child, go - be - tween of God,
2. Street child, beat child, no place left to go,
3. Grown child, old child, mem - ory full of years,
4. Spared child, spoiled child, hav - ing, want - ing more,
5. Hope - for - peace Child, God's stu - pend - ous sign,

love Child, Christ Child, heav - en's light - ning rod,
hurt child, used child, no one wants to know,
sad child, lost child, sto - ry told in tears,
wise child, faith child, know - ing joy in store,
down - to - earth Child, Star of stars that shine,

Refrain

This year, this year, let the day ar - rive when

Christ - mas comes for ev - ery - one, ev - ery - one a - live!

WORDS: Shirley Erena Murray (Matt. 2:1-12)
MUSIC: Carlton R. Young

STAR CHILD
45.45 with Refrain

© 1994 Hope Publishing Co.

2096 Rise Up, Shepherd, and Follow

(There's a Star in the East)

Leader

1. There's a star in the East on Christ-mas morn;
2. If you take good heed to the an-gel's words;

it will lead to the place where the
you'll for-get your flocks, you'll for-

All

rise up, shep-herd, and fol-low;

Christ was born;
get your herds;

rise up, shep-herd, and fol-low.

Refrain

Fol-low, fol-low, rise up, shep-herd, and fol-low,

WORDS: African American spiritual (Matt. 2:1-12; Luke 2:8-20)
MUSIC: African American spiritual

RISE UP, SHEPHERD
Irregular with Refrain

fol-low the star of Beth-le-hem. Rise up, shep-herd, and fol-low.

One Holy Night in Bethlehem   2097

1. One ho - ly night in Beth - le - hem the
2. Their mu - sic ech - oed through the town in -
3. As Jo - seph touched the lamb's soft wool and
4. Be still, and you will hear to - night these

air was filled with song. An - gel - ic voic - es
to the sta - ble stall, where Mar - y sang a
fed the don - key hay, he whis - tled his own
mel - o - dies of old. Then join your voice in

sang on high and shep - herds piped a - long:
lul - la - by and rocked her ba - by small:
hap - py tune and thanked God for this day:
har - mo - ny un - til the tale is told:

Refrain

Sing glo - ry, glo - ry, glo - ri - a! God's love is giv-en birth! Be

not a - fraid! Sing glo - ri - a, and peace to all the earth!

WORDS: Mary Nelson Keithahn (Luke 2:8-20)
MUSIC: John D. Horman

WHISTLER'S TUNE
CM with Refrain

2098   The Virgin Mary Had a Baby Boy

1. The vir - gin Ma - ry had a ba - by boy, the
2. The an - gels sang when the ba - by was born, the
3. The shep - herds came where the ba - by was born, the
4. The Wise Men came where the ba - by was born, the

vir - gin Ma - ry had a ba - by boy, the
an - gels sang when the ba - by was born, the
shep - herds came where the ba - by was born, the
Wise Men came where the ba - by was born, the

vir - gin Ma - ry had a ba - by boy,
an - gels sang when the ba - by was born,
shep - herds came where the ba - by was born,
Wise Men came where the ba - by was born, } and they

Refrain

say that his name is Je - sus. He come from the glo - ry,

he come from the glo - rious king-dom. He come from the

glo - ry, he come from the glo - rious king-dom. Oh,

yes! be - liev - er! Oh, yes! be - liev - er! He come from the

WORDS: West Indian carol (Matt. 2:1-12; Luke 2:1-20)   THE VIRGIN MARY
MUSIC: West Indian carol   10 10.10 9 with Refrain

glo - ry, he come from the glo - rious king - dom.

Joseph Dearest, Joseph Mine   2099

1. Jo - seph dear - est, Jo - seph mine, help me cra - dle the
2. Glad - ly, dear one, la - dy mine, help I cra - dle this
3. All shall come and bow the knee; wise and hap - py their

child di - vine; God re - ward thee and all that's thine in
child of thine; God's own light on us both shall shine in
souls shall be, lov - ing such a di - vin - i - ty, as

par - a - dise, so prays the moth - er Ma - ry.
par - a - dise, as prays the moth - er Ma - ry.
all may see in Je - sus, Son of Ma - ry.

Refrain

He came a - mong us at Christ - mas - time, at

Christ - mas - time, in Beth - le - hem; let us bring him from

far and wide Love's di - a - dem: Je - sus, Je - sus,

lo, he comes, and loves, and saves, and frees us!

WORDS: Trad. German (Luke 2:1-20)   JOSEPH LIEBER, JOSEPH MEIN
MUSIC: Trad. German   78.847 with Refrain

2100 Thou Didst Leave Thy Throne

1. Thou didst leave thy throne and thy king - ly crown,
2. Heav - en's arch - es rang when the an - gels sang,
3. The fox - es found rest, and the birds their nest
4. Thou camest, O Lord, with the liv - ing Word
5. When heav'ns arch - es shall ring and its choir shall sing

when thou cam - est to earth for me; but in
pro - claim - ing thy roy - al de - gree; but in
in the shade of the for - est tree; but thy
that should set thy peo - ple free; but with
at thy com - ing to vic - to - ry, let thy

Beth - le - hem's home there was found no room
low - ly birth didst thou come to earth,
couch was the sod, O thou Son of God,
mock - ing scorn, and with crown of thorn,
voice call me home, say - ing "Yet there is room,

WORDS: Emily E. S. Elliott
MUSIC: Timothy R. Matthews (Phil. 2:5-11)

MARGARET
Irregular

for thy ho - ly na - tiv - i - ty.
and in great hu - mil - i - ty.
in the des - erts of Gal - i - lee.
they bore thee to Cal - va - ry.
there is room at my side for thee!"

O come to my heart, Lord Je - sus,
O come to my heart, Lord Je - sus,
O come to my heart, Lord Je - sus,
O come to my heart, Lord Je - sus,
And my heart shall re - joice, Lord Je - sus,

there is room in my heart for thee.
there is room in my heart for thee.
there is room in my heart for thee.
there is room in my heart for thee.
when thou com - est and callest for me.

2101   Two Fishermen

1. Two fish - er - men, who lived a - long the
2. And as he walked a - long the shore 'twas
3. O Si - mon Pe - ter, An - drew, James, and
4. And you, good Chris - tians, one and all who'd

Sea of Gal - i - lee, stood by the shore to
James and John he'd find, and these two sons of
John be - lov - ed one, you heard Christ's call to
fol - low Je - sus' way, come leave be - hind what

cast their nets in - to an age - less sea. Now
Zeb - e - dee would leave their boats be - hind. Their
speak good news re - vealed to God's own Son. Su -
keeps you bound to trap - pings of our day, and

Je - sus watched them from a - far, then called them each by
work and all they held so dear they left be - side their
san - na, Ma - ry, Mag - da - lene who trav - eled with your
lis - ten as he calls your name to come and fol - low

name. It changed their lives, these sim - ple men; they'd
nets. Their names they'd heard as Je - sus called; they
Lord, you min - is - tered to him with joy for
near; for still he speaks in var - ied ways to

Refrain

nev - er be the same.
came with-out re - gret.   "Leave all things you have and
he is God a - dored.
those his call will hear.

WORDS: Suzanne Toolan (Matt. 4:18-22; Mark 1:16-20; Luke 5:1-11; 8:1-3)   LEAVE ALL THINGS BEHIND
MUSIC: Suzanne Toolan   CMD with Refrain

Words © 1986, music © 1970 GIA Publications, Inc.

come and fol - low me, and come and fol - low me."

Swiftly Pass the Clouds of Glory   2102

1. Swift - ly pass the clouds of glo - ry,
2. Glimpsed and gone the rev - e - la - tion,
3. Lord, trans - fig - ure our per - cep - tion

heav - en's voice, the dazz - ling light; Mo - ses and E -
they shall gain and keep its truth, not by build - ing
with the pur - est light that shines and re - cast our

li - jah van - ish; Christ a - lone com - mands the height!
on the moun - tain an - y shrine or sa - cred booth,
life's in - ten - tions to the shape of your de - signs,

Pe - ter, James, and John fall si - lent,
but by fol - low - ing the Sav - ior
til we seek no oth - er glo - ry

turn - ing from the sum - mit's rise down - ward toward the
through the val - ley to the cross and by test - ing
than what lies past Cal - vary's hill and our liv - ing

shad - owed val - ley where their Lord has fixed his eyes.
faith's re - sil - ience through be - tray - al, pain, and loss.
and our dy - ing and our ris - ing by your will.

WORDS: Thomas H. Troeger (Matt. 17:1-8; Mark 9:2-8; Luke 9:28-36)
MUSIC: George Henry Day

GENEVA
87.87 D

2103 We Have Come at Christ's Own Bidding

1. We have come at Christ's own bid-ding to this
2. Light breaks through our clouds and shad-ows, splen - dor
3. Strength-ened by this glimpse of glo - ry, fear - ful

high and ho - ly place, where we wait with
bathes the flesh - joined Word, Mo - ses and E -
lest our faith de - cline, we, like Pe - ter,

hope and long - ing for some to - ken of God's grace.
li - jah mar - vel as the heaven-ly voice is heard.
find it tempt-ing to re - main and build a shrine.

Here we pray for new as - sur - ance that our faith is
Eyes and hearts be - hold with won - der how the Law and
But true wor - ship gives us cour - age to pro - claim what

WORDS: Carl P. Daw, Jr. (Matt. 17:1-8; Mark 9:2-8; Luke 9:28-36)
MUSIC: Rowland H. Prichard; arr. by Ralph Vaughan Williams

HYFRYDOL
87.87D

Words © 1988 Hope Publishing Co.

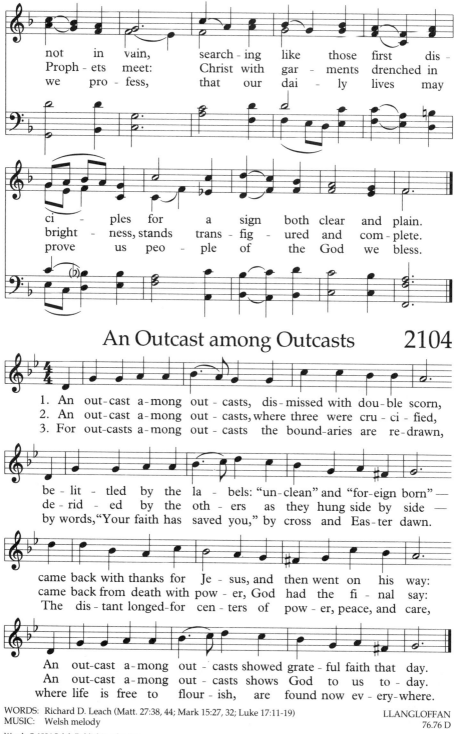

not in vain,   search - ing   like   those   first   dis -
Proph - ets   meet: Christ with   gar   -   ments   drenched in
we   pro - fess,   that   our   dai   -   ly   lives   may

ci   -   ples   for   a   sign   both   clear   and   plain.
bright   -   ness, stands   trans - fig   -   ured and   com - plete.
prove   us   peo - ple   of   the   God   we   bless.

An Outcast among Outcasts   2104

1. An out-cast a-mong out - casts, dis-missed with dou-ble scorn,
2. An out-cast a-mong out - casts, where three were cru - ci - fied,
3. For out-casts a-mong out - casts   the bound-aries are re-drawn,

be - lit - tled   by the   la - bels: "un-clean" and "for-eign born" —
de - rid - ed   by the   oth - ers   as they hung side by side —
by words, "Your faith has   saved you," by cross   and Eas-ter dawn.

came back with thanks for   Je - sus, and   then went on   his   way:
came back from death with pow - er, God   had   the   fi - nal   say:
The   dis - tant longed-for   cen - ters of   pow - er, peace, and care,

An   out-cast a-mong   out - casts showed grate - ful faith that   day.
An   out-cast a-mong   out - casts shows God   to   us   to - day.
where life   is   free   to   flour - ish,   are   found now ev - ery-where.

WORDS: Richard D. Leach (Matt. 27:38, 44; Mark 15:27, 32; Luke 17:11-19)   LLANGLOFFAN
MUSIC: Welsh melody   76.76 D

Words © 1994 Selah Publishing Co., Inc.

2105   Jesus, Tempted in the Desert

1. Je - sus, tempt - ed in the des - ert,
2. Je - sus, tempt - ed at the tem - ple,
3. Je - sus, tempt - ed on the moun - tain
4. When we face temp - ta - tion's pow - er,

lone - ly, hun - gry, filled with dread: "Use your power," the
high a - bove its an - cient wall: "Throw your - self from
by the lure of vast do - main: "Fall be - fore me!
lone - ly, strug - gling, filled with dread, Christ, who knew the

tempt - er tells him; "Turn these bar - ren
loft - y tur - ret; an - gels wait to
Be my ser - vant! Glo - ry, fame, you're
tempt - er's ho - ur, come and be our

rocks to bread!" "Not a - lone by bread," he an - swers,
break your fall!" Je - sus shuns such emp - ty mar - vels,
sure to gain!" Je - sus sees the dazz - ling vi - sion,
liv - ing bread. By your grace, pro - tect, pre - serve us

WORDS: Herman G. Stuempfle, Jr. (Matt. 4:1-11; Luke 4:1-13)
MUSIC: Thomas J. Williams

EBENEZER
87.87 D

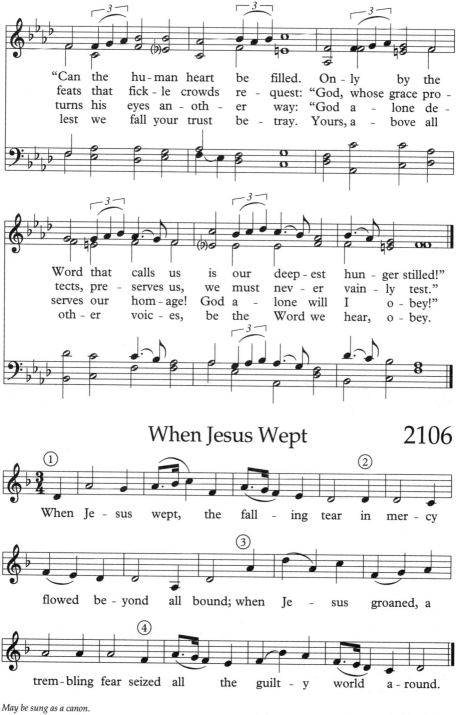

"Can the hu-man heart be filled. On-ly by the
feats that fick-le crowds re-quest: "God, whose grace pro-
turns his eyes an-oth-er way: "God a-lone de-
lest we fall your trust be-tray. Yours, a-bove all

Word that calls us is our deep-est hun-ger stilled!"
tects, pre-serves us, we must nev-er vain-ly test."
serves our hom-age! God a-lone will I o-bey!"
oth-er voic-es, be the Word we hear, o-bey.

When Jesus Wept   2106

When Je-sus wept, the fall-ing tear in mer-cy

flowed be-yond all bound; when Je-sus groaned, a

trem-bling fear seized all the guilt-y world a-round.

May be sung as a canon.

WORDS: William Billings (John 11:35)   WHEN JESUS WEPT
MUSIC: William Billings   LM

2107 Wade in the Water

WORDS: African American spiritual (John 5:2-9)
MUSIC: African American spiritual; arr. by Carl Haywood

WADE IN THE WATER
Irregular with Refrain

Arr. © 1992 Carl Haywood

CHRIST'S LIFE AND TEACHING, *see further:*

2278 The Lord's Prayer

O How He Loves You and Me   2108

1. O how he loves you and me!____ O how he loves you and me!____ He gave his life. What more could he give? O how he loves you; O how he loves me; O how he loves you and me!____

2. Je - sus to Cal - v'ry did go;____ his love for sin - ners to show.____ What he did there brought hope from de - spair. O how he loves you; O how he loves me; O how he loves you and me!____

WORDS: Kurt Kaiser (1 John 3:1)
MUSIC: Kurt Kaiser

PATRICIA
Irregular

2109   Hosanna! Hosanna!

1. Je - sus rode in - to Je - ru - sa - lem.
2. Ev - ery - bod - y brought their hopes and dreams.

Ho -

All the peo - ple sang their
Life just is - n't al - ways

san - na! Ho - san - na!

praise to him.
what it seems.

Ho - san - na! Ho - san - na!

Came to town up-on a don - key's back;
Need some-bod - y who can help us be

Ho - san - na! Ho -

seemed so low - ly but he's Lord in fact.
lib - er - at - ed from cap - tiv - i - ty.

san - na!

Ho -

WORDS: Cathy Townley (Matt. 21:6-16; Mark 11:7-10; Luke 19:35-38)
MUSIC: Cathy Townley

© 1993 Abingdon Press, admin. by The Copyright Co.

HOSANNA! HOSANNA!
Irregular with Refrain

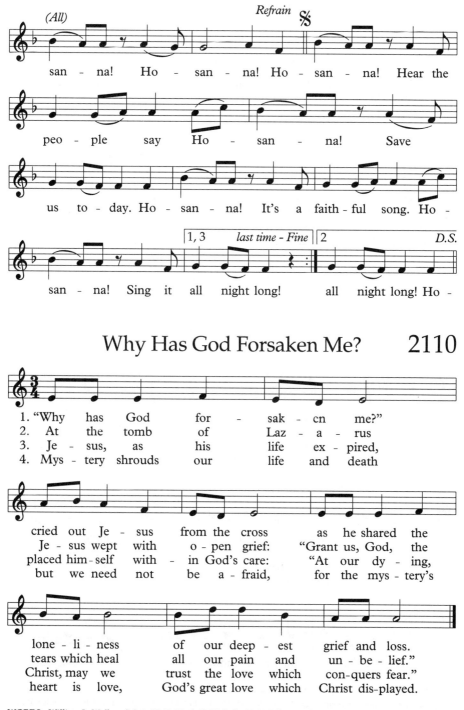

(All) Refrain %

san - na! Ho - san - na! Ho - san - na! Hear the

peo - ple say Ho - san - na! Save

us to - day. Ho - san - na! It's a faith - ful song. Ho -

|1, 3 *last time - Fine* |2 D.S.

san - na! Sing it all night long! all night long! Ho -

Why Has God Forsaken Me? 2110

1. "Why has God for - sak - en me?"
2. At the tomb of Laz - a - rus
3. Je - sus, as his life ex - pired,
4. Mys - tery shrouds our life and death

cried out Je - sus from the cross as he shared the
Je - sus wept with o - pen grief: "Grant us, God, the
placed him - self with - in God's care: "At our dy - ing,
but we need not be a - fraid, for the mys - tery's

lone - li - ness of our deep - est grief and loss.
tears which heal all our pain and un - be - lief."
Christ, may we trust the love which con - quers fear."
heart is love, God's great love which Christ dis - played.

WORDS: William L. Wallace (Matt. 27:46; Mark 15:34; Luke 23:46; John 11:35) SHIMPI
MUSIC: Taihei Sato 77.77

Words © 1981 William L. Wallace; music © 1983 Taihei Sato

2111 We Sang Our Glad Hosannas

1. We sang our glad ho - san - nas and waved our branch-es
(2. We) heard an an - gry Je - sus in Tem - ple courts de -
(3. We) served him at the ta - ble with wine, un - leav-ened
(4. We) saw a suf-fering Je - sus a - lone, with - out a

high, but some were si - lent, frown - ing, as
clare, "Be gone, you mon - ey chang - ers! This
bread. "The one who will be - tray me now
friend, and heard the voic - es shout - ing a -

Je - sus rode on by. They sought a roy - al
is a house of prayer." Though man - y came for
eats with me," he said. His friends would not be -
buse un - til the end. We wept as we stood

Sav - ior, but did not un - der-stand a king could rule by
heal - ing and stayed to hear his word, still oth - ers, hos - tile,
lieve him, but one by one that night, as sol - diers came to
watch-ing Love's light grow dim and die, and cried, "Why did this

1-3

lov - ing in - stead of by com - mand. 2. We
plot - ted and thus his death as - sured. 3. We
take him, they scur - ried out of sight. 4. We
hap - pen? God, tell us, tell us

4

why!" *5. We bu - ried him, not know - ing that

*St. 5 for Easter Sunday. Sts. 1-4 for Palm/Passion Sunday or Holy Week

WORDS: Mary Nelson Keithahn (Matt. 21:1-17; 27:27-31, 55-56; Mark 11:15-19; 14:17-21, 43-50;   HOLY WEEK
      John 19:38-42; 20:1-18)   76.76 D
MUSIC: John D. Horman

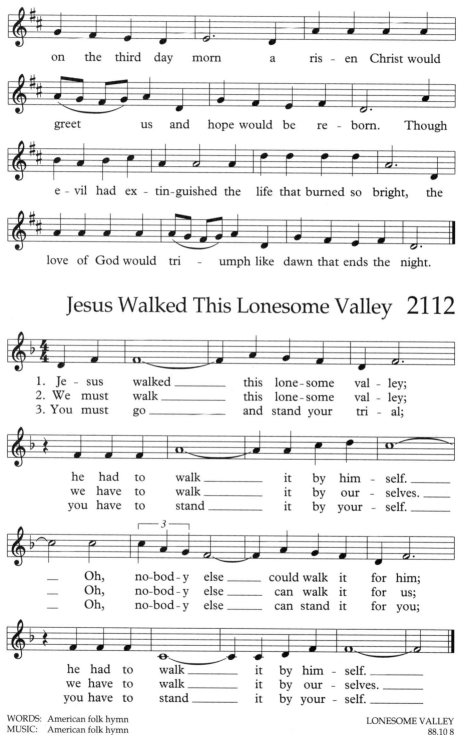

on the third day morn a - ris - en Christ would

greet us and hope would be re - born. Though

e - vil had ex - tin-guished the life that burned so bright, the

love of God would tri - umph like dawn that ends the night.

Jesus Walked This Lonesome Valley 2112

1. Je - sus walked _____ this lone - some val - ley;
2. We must walk _____ this lone - some val - ley;
3. You must go _____ and stand your tri - al;

he had to walk _____ it by him - self. _____
we have to walk _____ it by our - selves. _____
you have to stand _____ it by your - self. _____

— Oh, no - bod - y else _____ could walk it for him;
— Oh, no - bod - y else _____ can walk it for us;
— Oh, no - bod - y else _____ can stand it for you;

he had to walk _____ it by him - self. _____
we have to walk _____ it by our - selves. _____
you have to stand _____ it by your - self. _____

WORDS: American folk hymn
MUSIC: American folk hymn

LONESOME VALLEY
88.10 8

2113

Lamb of God

1. Your on - ly Son, no sin to hide, but you have
2. Your gift of love, they cru - ci - fied, they laughed and
3. I was so lost, I should have died, but you have

sent him from your side, to walk up - on this guilt - y
scorned him as he died, the hum - ble king they named a
brought me to your side, to be led by your staff and

| 1 | 2, 3 |

sod, and to be - come the Lamb of God. _____
fraud and sac - ri - ficed the Lamb of God.
rod, and to be called a lamb of God.

Refrain

O Lamb of God, sweet Lamb of God, I love the

ho - ly Lamb of God! O wash me in his pre - cious

blood — my Je - sus Christ, the Lamb of God.

WORDS: Twila Paris (Ps. 23:1, 4-5; Matt. 27:37-44; Mark 15:26-32; Luke 23:35-38)
MUSIC: Twila Paris

SWEET LAMB OF GOD
Irregular with Refrain

At the Font We Start Our Journey 2114

1. At the font we start our jour - ney, in the Eas-ter
2. At the pul - pit we are fash - ioned by the Eas-ter
3. At the al - tar we are nour - ished with the Eas-ter
4. At the door we are com - mis - sioned, now the Eas-ter

faith bap - tized; doubts and fears no long - er blind us,
tale re - told in - to wit - nes - ses and proph-ets,
gift of bread; in our break-ing it to piec - es
vic - tory's won, to re - store a world di - vid - ed

by the light of Christ sur - prised. Al - le - lu - ia!
by the power of Christ made bold. Al - le - lu - ia!
see the love of Christ out - spread. Al - le - lu - ia!
to the peace of Christ as one. Al - le - lu - ia!

Al - le - lu - ia! Hope held out and re - al - ized.
Al - le - lu - ia! Faith pro - claimed, yet still un - told.
Al - le - lu - ia! Life em - braced, yet free - ly shed.
Al - le - lu - ia! Eas - ter's work must still be done.

WORDS: Jeffery Rowthorn (Acts 10:36-43; Col. 3:15)
MUSIC: John Goss

LAUDA ANIMA
87.87.87

2115 Christ Has Risen

1. Christ has ris - en while earth slum - bers,
Christ has ris - en where hope died, as he said and
as he prom - ised, as we doubt - ed
and de - nied. Let the moon em - brace the bless - ing;

2. Christ has ris - en for the peo - ple
whom he died to love and save; Christ has ris - en
for the wom - en bring - ing flowers to
grace his grave. Christ has ris - en for dis - ci - ples

3. Christ has ris - en to com - pan - ion
for - mer friends who fear the night, sens - ing loss and
lim - i - ta - tion where their faith had
once burned bright. They be - moan what is no long - er,

4. Christ has ris - en and for - ev - er
lives to chal - lenge and to change all whose lives are
messed or man - gled, all who find re -
li - gion strange. Christ is ris - en, Christ is pres - ent

WORDS: John Bell (Matt. 28; Mark 16; Luke 24; John 20–21; 1 Cor. 15:3-8)
MUSIC: William Moore

HOLY MANNA
87.87 D

Words © 1988 WGRG The Iona Community (Scotland), admin. by GIA Publications, Inc.

let the sun sus - tain the cheer; let the world con -
hud - dled in an up - stairs room. He whose word in -
they ex - pect no hope - ful sign till Christ ends their
mak - ing us what he has been — ev - i - dence of

firm the ru - mor: Christ is ris - en, God is here!
spired cre - a - tion can't be si - lenced by the tomb.
con - ver - sa - tion, break - ing bread and shar - ing wine.
trans - for - ma - tion in which God is known and seen.

Christ the Lord Is Risen   2116

1. Christ the Lord is risen! Christ the Lord is risen! Ye - su.

Christ the Lord is risen! Christ the Lord is risen! Ye - su.

2. He has conquered death ...
3. Sin has done its worst ...
4. He is King of kings ...
5. He is Lord of lords ...

6. All the world is his ...
7. Come and worship him ...
8. Christ our Lord is risen! ...
9. Hallelujah! ...

WORDS: Tom Colvin (1 Cor. 15:20-22, 26-28, 54-57; Rev. 17:14)
MUSIC: Ghanian folk song; adapt. by Tom Colvin; arr. by Kevin R. Hackett

GARU
552.552

Words, adapt., and arr. © 1969 Hope Publishing Co.

2117 Spirit of God

1. Spir-it of God, bright Wind, breath that bids life
2. Spir-it of God, bright Dove, grant us your peace
3. Spir-it of God, bright Hands, e - ven in far -
4. Spir-it of God, bright Flame, send us in your ho -
5. Spir-it of God in all, we glad-ly hear

be - gin, blow as you al - ways do; cre -
and love, heal-ing up - on your wings for
off lands you hold all the hu - man race in
ly name, the pow-er to heal, to share your
your call, the life in our hands that sings, the

ate us a - new. _____ Give us the breath
all liv-ing things. _____ For when we live
one warm em - brace. _____ No mat-ter where
love ev-ery-where. _____ We can-not fail
power of your wings. _____ Born of your grace

to sing, lift - ed on soar - ing wing,)
your peace, cap-tives will find re - lease,)
we go, you hold us to - geth - er so,)
or fall, or know de - feat at all,)
we rise, love shin-ing in our eyes,)

held in your hands, _____ borne on your wings. _

Refrain

Al - le - lu - ia!

[1] [2]

Come, Spir - it, come! ___ come! _____

WORDS: Steve Garnaas-Holmes (Gen. 1:2; Matt. 3:16-17; Luke 3:22; Acts 2:1-4)   DOVE SONG
MUSIC: Steve Garnaas-Holmes   Irregular with Refrain

© 1987 Steve Garnaas-Holmes

Holy Spirit, Come to Us

(Veni Sancte Spiritus)

2118

Repeat as desired.

Ho - ly Spir - it, come to us. ____
Ve - ni Sanc - te Spir - i - tus. ____

WORDS: Pentecost Sequence; adapt. by Jacques Berthier
MUSIC: Jacques Berthier

VENI SANCTE SPIRITUS
Irregular

Where the Spirit of the Lord Is

2119

Where the Spir-it of the Lord is, there is peace; where the

Spir-it of the Lord is, there is love. There is

com-fort in life's dark-est hour; there is light and life, there is

help and pow-er in the Spir-it, in the Spir-it of the Lord. ____

WORDS: Stephen R. Adams (2 Cor. 3:17)
MUSIC: Stephen R. Adams

ADAMS
Irregular

2120 Spirit, Spirit of Gentleness

Refrain

Spir - it, Spir - it of gen - tle-ness, blow through the

wil - der-ness call - ing and free; _____ Spir -

it, Spir - it of rest - less-ness, stir me from plac - id-ness,

Fine

Wind, Wind on the sea. _____

1. You moved on the wa - ters, you called to the
2. You swept through the des - ert, you stung with the
3. You sang in a sta - ble, you cried from a
4. You call from to - mor - row, you break an - cient

deep, _____ then you coaxed up the moun - tains from the
sand, _____ and you goad - ed your peo - ple with a
hill, _____ then you whis-pered in si - lence when the
schemes, _____ from the bon - dage of sor - row the

val - leys of sleep; _____ and o - ver the e - ons you
law and a land; _____ and when they were blind - ed with their
whole world was still; _____ and down in the cit - y you
cap - tives dream dreams, _ our wom - en see vi - sions, our

called to each thing: _____ _____ wake from your slum -
i - dols and lies, _____ then you spoke through your proph -
called once a - gain, _____ when you blew through your peo -
men clear their eyes, _____ with bold new de - ci -

WORDS: James K. Manley (Gen. 1:2; Luke 2:7-14; Acts 2:1-4)
MUSIC: James K. Manley

SPIRIT OF GENTLENESS
Irregular with Refrain

© 1978 James K. Manley

D.C.

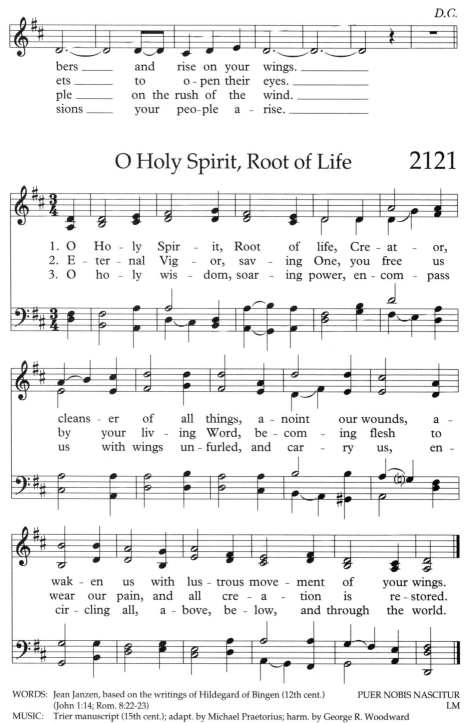

bers _____ and rise on your wings. _____
ets _____ to o - pen their eyes. _____
ple _____ on the rush of the wind. _____
sions _____ your peo - ple a - rise. _____

O Holy Spirit, Root of Life   2121

1. O Ho - ly Spir - it, Root of life, Cre - at - or,
2. E - ter - nal Vig - or, sav - ing One, you free us
3. O ho - ly wis - dom, soar - ing power, en - com - pass

cleans - er of all things, a - noint our wounds, a -
by your liv - ing Word, be - com - ing flesh to
us with wings un - furled, and car - ry us, en -

wak - en us with lus - trous move - ment of your wings.
wear our pain, and all cre - a - tion is re - stored.
cir - cling all, a - bove, be - low, and through the world.

WORDS: Jean Janzen, based on the writings of Hildegard of Bingen (12th cent.)   PUER NOBIS NASCITUR
       (John 1:14; Rom. 8:22-23)   LM
MUSIC: Trier manuscript (15th cent.); adapt. by Michael Praetorius; harm. by George R. Woodward
Words © 1991 Abingdon Press, admin. by The Copyright Co.

2122 She Comes Sailing on the Wind

Refrain

She comes sail-ing on the wind, her wings flash-ing in the sun; on a jour-ney just be-gun, she flies on. And in the pas-sage of her flight, her song rings out through the night, full of laugh-ter, full of light, she flies on.

Fine

1. ____ Si - lent wa - ters rock - ing on the morn-ing of our birth, like an emp - ty cra - dle wait - ing to be filled. ____ And from the heart of God the Spir - it moved up - on the earth, like a moth - er breath-ing

2. ____ Ma - ny were the dream-ers whose eyes were giv - en sight when the Spir - it filled their dreams with life and form. ____ ____ Des-erts turned to gar - dens, bro - ken hearts found new de - light, and then down the a - ges

3. To a gen - tle girl in Gal - i - lee, a gen - tle breeze she came, a whis - per soft - ly call - ing in the dark, ____ the prom-ise of a child of peace whose reign would nev - er end, Ma - ry sang the Spir - it

4. ____ Fly - ing to the riv - er, she wait - ed cir - cling high a - bove the child now grown so full of grace. ____ As he rose up from the wa - ter, she swept down from the sky, and she car - ried him a -

5. Long af - ter the deep dark-ness that fell up - on the world, af - ter dawn re - turned in flame of ris - ing sun, ____ the Spir - it touched the earth a - gain, a - gain, her wings un - furled, bring - ing life in wind and

WORDS: Gordon Light (Gen. 1:2; Matt. 3:16-17; Mark 1:10-11; Luke 1:26-56; 3:22; Acts 2:1-4) SHE FLIES ON
MUSIC: Gordon Light Irregular with Refrain

life in-to her child. ____
still she flew on. ____ She comes
song with-in her heart. ____
way in her em- brace. ____ She comes
fire as she flew on. ____ She comes

Loving Spirit 2123

1., 5. Lov - ing Spir - it, lov - ing Spir - it, you have
2. Like a moth - er you en - fold me, hold my
3. Like a fa - ther you pro - tect me, teach me
4. Friend and lov - er, in your close - ness I am

cho - sen me to be — you have drawn me to your
life with - in your own, feed me with your ver - y
the dis - cern - ing eye, hoist me up up - on your
known and held and blessed: In your prom - ise is my

won - der, you have set your sign on me.
bod - y, form me of your flesh and bone.
shoul - der, let me see the world from high.
com - fort, in your pres-ence I may rest.

WORDS: Shirley Erena Murray
MUSIC: V. Earle Copes
KINGDOM
87.87

Words © 1987 The Hymn Society, admin. by Hope Publishing Co.

2124 Come, O Holy Spirit, Come
(Wa Wa Wa Emimimo)

Leader

Ho - ly Spir - it, come.
E - mi - o - lo - ye.

All

Come, O Ho - ly Spir - it, come,
Wa wa wa E - mi - mi - mo,

al - might - y Spir - it, come.
A - lag - ba - ra - me - ta.

Come, al - might - y Spir - it, come,
Wa wa wa A - lag - ba - ra,

O Spir - it, come.
E - mi - mi - mo.

Come, come, come.
Wa - o wa - o wa - o.

WORDS: Original Yoruba; English trans. by I-to Loh
MUSIC: Trad. Yoruba as taught by Samuel Solanke (Nigeria)

WA EMIMIMO
Irregular

English trans. © 1995 General Board of Global Ministries, GBGMusik

2125 Come, Holy Spirit

Part 2 (descant)

Hear us call - ing,

Part 1 (melody)

Come, Ho - ly Spir - it. Come, Ho - ly

WORDS: Mark Foreman
MUSIC: Mark Foreman

FOREMAN
Irregular

© 1982 Mercy/Vineyard Publishing

2126

All Who Hunger

1. All who hun-ger, gath-er glad-ly; ho-ly man-na
2. All who hun-ger, nev-er strang-ers; seek-er, be a
3. All who hun-ger, sing to-geth-er; Je-sus Christ is

is our bread. Come from wil-der-ness and wan-dering.
wel-come guest. Come from rest-less-ness and roam-ing.
liv-ing bread. Come from lone-li-ness and long-ing.

Here, in truth, we will be fed. You that yearn for
Here, in joy, we keep the feast. We that once were
Here, in peace, we have been led. Blest are those who

days of full-ness, all a-round us is our food.
lost and scat-tered in com-mu-nion's love have stood.
from this ta-ble live their lives in grat-i-tude.

WORDS: Sylvia G. Dunstan (Exod. 16:13-15; Ps. 34:8; John 4:10; 1 Cor. 5:8)
MUSIC: William Moore

HOLY MANNA
87.87 D

Taste and see the grace e - ter - nal. Taste and see that God is good.

Come and See

2127

(Kyrie)

1. "Come and see, come and see, I am the way and the truth," said he.
2. Ky - ri - e, Ky - ri - e, Ky - ri - e e - le - i - son.

"Fol - low me, fol - low me, come as a child, O come and see." _ *(to 2.)*
Chris - te, Chris - te, Chris - te e - le - i - son. _ *(to 3.)*

Part 2 (descant)

3. Chris - te,* Chris - te, a - do - ra - mus te.

Part 1 (melody)

(2.) Ky - ri - e,* Ky - ri - e, Ky - ri - e e - le - i - son.

Al - le - lu - ia, Ky - ri - e e - le - i - son.

Chris - te, Chris - te, Chris - te e - le - i - son.

Translation: Christ, we adore you. Alleluia, Lord have mercy.
Lord, have mercy. Christ, have mercy.

WORDS: Marilyn Houser Hamm (John 1:35-51; 14:6)
MUSIC: Marilyn Houser Hamm

MH KYRIE
Irregular

© 1974 Marilyn Houser Hamm

2128 Come and Find the Quiet Center

1. Come and find the qui - et cen - ter in the crowd-ed life we
2. Si - lence is a friend who claims us, cools the heat and slows the
3. In the Spir - it let us trav - el, o - pen to each oth - er's

lead, find the room for hope to en - ter, find the
pace, God it is who speaks and names us, knows our
pain, let our loves and fears un - rav - el, cel - e -

frame where we are freed: Clear the cha - os and the
be - ing, touch-es base, mak - ing space with - in our
brate the space we gain: There's a place for deep-est

clut - ter, clear our eyes that we can see all the
think - ing, lift - ing shades to show the sun, rais - ing
dream - ing, there's a time for heart to care, in the

things that real - ly mat - ter, be at peace, and sim-ply be.
cour - age when we're shrink-ing, find-ing scope for faith be - gun.
Spir - it's live - ly schem-ing there is al - ways room to spare.

WORDS: Shirley Erena Murray
MUSIC: Attr. to B. F. White

BEACH SPRING
87.87 D

Words © 1992 Hope Publishing Co.

2129 I Have Decided to Follow Jesus

1. I have de - cid - ed to fol-low Je - sus, I have de -

cid - ed to fol-low Je - sus, I have de - cid - ed to fol-low

2. The world behind me, the cross before me ...
3. Though none go with me, still I will follow ...

WORDS: Anon.
MUSIC: Anon.

ASSAM
10 10.10 8

The Summons

2130

1. Will you come and fol-low me if I but call
2. Will you leave your-self be-hind if I but call
3. Will you let the blind-ed see if I but call
4. Will you love the "you" you hide if I but call
5. Lord, your sum-mons ech-oes true when you but call

your name? _____ Will you go where you don't know and
your name? _____ Will you care for cruel and kind and
your name? _____ Will you set the pris-oners free and
your name? _____ Will you quell the fear in-side and
my name. _____ Let me turn and fol-low you and

nev-er be the same? _____ Will you let my love be
nev-er be the same? _____ Will you risk the hos-tile
nev-er be the same? _____ Will you kiss the lep-er
nev-er be the same? _____ Will you use the faith you've
nev-er be the same. _____ In your com-pa-ny I'll

shown, __ will you let my name be known, _ will you
stare _____ should your life at-tract or scare? __ Will you
clean, __ and do such as this un-seen, _____ and ad-
found __ to re-shape the world a-round, _ through my
go _____ where your love and foot-steps show. __ Thus I'll

let my life be grown in you and you in me? _____
let me an-swer prayer in you and you in me? _____
mit to what I mean in you and you in me? _____
sight and touch and sound in you and you in me? _____
move and live and grow in you and you in me. _____

WORDS: John Bell
MUSIC: Traditional Scottish

KELVINGROVE
13 13 7 7 13

Words © 1987 WGRG The Iona Community (Scotland), admin. by GIA Publications, Inc.

2131 Humble Thyself in the Sight of the Lord

WORDS: Bob Hudson (James 4:10)
MUSIC: Bob Hudson

HUMBLE THYSELF
Irregular

You Who Are Thirsty

You who are thirst-y, come to the well and drink from wa-ters flow - ing. You who are hun-gry, come to the bread and eat of his ho - li-ness. You who are tired, find rest. You who are weak, find strength. You who are thirst-y, come to the well and drink.

[1]

drink.

[2] He will free - ly feed all of them who are weak. He will quench the righ-teous thirst of all who hum-bly seek.

Repeat ending D.C. | Song ending

seek. _____

WORDS: Barbara Ross (Isa. 55:1; Matt. 5:6; 11:28)
MUSIC: Barbara Ross

ALL WHO HUMBLY SEEK
Irregular

INVITATION, *see further:*
2106   When Jesus Wept

2133   Give Me a Clean Heart

Give me a clean heart so I may serve thee. Lord, fix my heart so that I may be used by thee. For I'm not worth - y of all those bless - ings. Give me a clean heart, ____ and I'll fol - low thee. _____

WORDS: Margaret P. Douroux (Ps. 51:10)   DOUROUX
MUSIC: Margaret P. Douroux   Irregular

© 1970 Margaret P. Douroux

2134   Forgive Us, Lord
(Perdón, Señor)

Leader

1. For griev-ance and in - jus - tice:
2. For weak-ness and trans-gres - sion:
3. In your e - ter - nal mer - cy:

1. *Por tan - tas in - jus - ti - cias:*
2. *Por to - das nues-tras fal - tas:*
3. *En tu mi - se - ri - cor - dia:*

All   *Fine*

For-give us, Lord.   For -
Per - dón, Se - ñor.   *Per -*

WORDS: Jorge Lockward; English trans. by Raquel Mora Martínez (Ps. 51:1-3)   CONFESIÓN
MUSIC: Jorge Lockward   4.74.74

© 1996 Abingdon Press, admin. by The Copyright Co.

D.C.

A - loof-ness and in - dif-ference:
Re - sis-tance and re - bel - lion:
In your sus - tain-ing grace:
Por tan-ta in - di - fe - ren - cia:
Por nues - tra re - bel - di - a:
en tu di - vi - na gra - cia:

D.C.

give us, Lord.
dón, Se - ñor.

For-give us, Lord.
Per-dón, Se - ñor.

When Cain Killed Abel

2135

1. When Cain killed A - bel in a fight, and
2. In ev - ery fam - ily, small or great, when
3. And when in church and world to - day such
4. Good Chris - tians, join in God's la - ment, weep

Ja - cob stole an - oth - er's right, when Jo - seph's broth - ers
jeal - ou - sy twists love to hate, and ri - vals turn to
feel - ings still come in - to play, when broth - ers, sis - ters
now and mourn, be pen - i - tent, and pray to God: For -

gave him chase, God wept and mourned their fall from grace.
en - e - mies, God weeps at our hos - til - i - ties.
stand a - part, God weeps for ev - ery bro - ken heart.
give us all. Re - store us as be - fore the fall.

WORDS: Mary Nelson Keithahn (Gen. 4:8-10; 27; 37)
MUSIC: John D. Horman

AFTER THE FALL
LM

Words © 1998, music © 2000 Abingdon Press, admin. by The Copyright Co.

2136   Out of the Depths

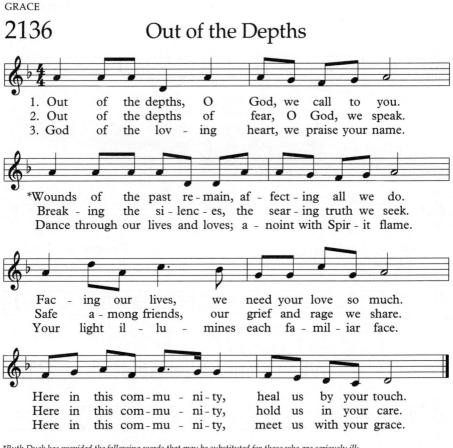

1. Out of the depths, O God, we call to you.
2. Out of the depths of fear, O God, we speak.
3. God of the lov - ing heart, we praise your name.

*Wounds of the past re - main, af - fect - ing all we do.
Break - ing the si - lenc - es, the sear - ing truth we seek.
Dance through our lives and loves; a - noint with Spir - it flame.

Fac - ing our lives, we need your love so much.
Safe a - mong friends, our grief and rage we share.
Your light il - lu - mines each fa - mil - iar face.

Here in this com - mu - ni - ty, heal us by your touch.
Here in this com - mu - ni - ty, hold us in your care.
Here in this com - mu - ni - ty, meet us with your grace.

Ruth Duck has provided the following words that may be substituted for those who are seriously ill:
Free us from fear of death, our faith and hope renew …

or, for those who have been abused:
Wounds of abuse remain, affecting all we do …

WORDS: Ruth Duck (Ps. 130:1)
MUSIC: Robert J. Batastini

FENNVILLE
10 12.10 12

Words © 1988, music © 1994 GIA Publications, Inc.

2137   Would I Have Answered When You Called

1. Would I have an - swered when you called, "Come,
2. Would I have fol - lowed where you led through
3. Would I have matched my step with yours when
4. O Christ, I can - not search my heart through

WORDS: Herman G. Stuempfle, Jr. (Matt. 4:12-23; 26:56; Mark 1:16-20; 14:50; Luke 5:1-11)
MUSIC: Trad. English melody

KINGSFOLD
CMD

Words © 1997 GIA Publications, Inc.

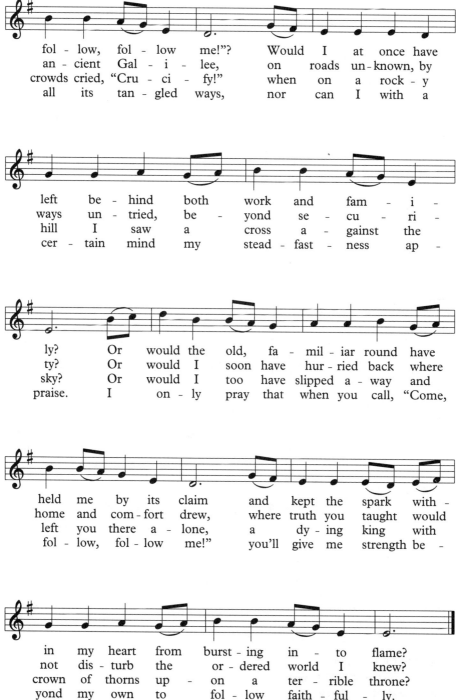

fol - low, fol - low me!"? Would I at once have
an - cient Gal - i - lee, on roads un - known, by
crowds cried, "Cru - ci - fy!" when on a rock - y
all its tan - gled ways, nor can I with a

left be - hind both work and fam - i -
ways un - tried, be - yond se - cu - ri -
hill I saw a cross a - gainst the
cer - tain mind my stead - fast - ness ap -

ly? Or would the old, fa - mil - iar round have
ty? Or would I soon have hur - ried back where
sky? Or would I too have slipped a - way and
praise. I on - ly pray that when you call, "Come,

held me by its claim and kept the spark with -
home and com - fort drew, where truth you taught would
left you there a - lone, a dy - ing king with
fol - low, fol - low me!" you'll give me strength be -

in my heart from burst - ing in - to flame?
not dis - turb the or - dered world I knew?
crown of thorns up - on a ter - rible throne?
yond my own to fol - low faith - ful - ly.

2138 Sunday's Palms Are Wednesday's Ashes

1. *Sun-day's palms are Wednes-day's ash - es as an -
2. We have failed to love our neigh - bors, their of -
3. We are hast - y to judge oth - ers, blind to

oth - er Lent be - gins; thus we kneel be - fore our
fenc - es to for - give, have not lis - tened to their
proof of hu - man need; and our lack of un - der -

Mak - er in con - tri - tion for our
trou - bles, nor have cared just how they
stand - ing dem - on - strates our in - ner

sins. We have marred bap - tis - mal pledg - es, in re -
live, we are jeal - ous, proud, im - pa - tient, lov - ing
greed; we have wast - ed earth's re - sourc - es; want and

bel - lion gone a - stray; now, re - turn - ing, seek for -
o - ver - much our things; may the yield - ing of our
suf - fering we've ig - nored; come and cleanse us, then re -

give - ness; grant us par - don, God, this day!
fail - ings be our Len - ten of - fer - ings.
store us; make new hearts with - in us, Lord!

*The first line of the hymn recalls the custom of burning remaining palm leaves of the previous year to form the ashes for this observance.

WORDS: Rae E. Whitney
MUSIC: Attr. to B. F. White

BEACH SPRING
87.87 D

Words © 1991 Selah Publishing Co., Inc.

REPENTANCE, *see further:*

2275   Kyrie (Dvořák/Schram)
2277   Lord, Have Mercy

Oh, I Know the Lord's Laid His Hands on Me

2139

Oh, I know the Lord, I know the Lord,
I know the Lord's laid his hands on me. Oh, hands on me.

Leader

1. Did ev-er you see the like be-fore?
   King Je-sus preach-ing to the poor!
2. Oh, was-n't that a hap-py day
   when Je-sus washed my sins a-way!
3. __ Some seek the Lord and don't seek him right;
   they fool all day and pray at night,
4. __ My Lord's done just what he said;
   he's healed the sick and raised the dead;

All

I know the Lord's laid his hands on me; hands on me. Oh,

WORDS: African American spiritual
MUSIC: African American spiritual

I KNOW
Irregular with Refrain

2140 Since Jesus Came into My Heart

1. What a won-der-ful change in my life has been wrought
2. I have ceased from my wand-ering and go-ing a-stray,
3. I'm pos-sessed of a hope that is stead-fast and sure,
4. There's a light in the val-ley of death now for me,
5. I shall go there to dwell in that Cit-y, I know,

since Je-sus came in-to my heart!

I have
And my
And no
And the
And I'm

light in my soul for which long I had sought,
sins, which were man-y, are all washed a-way,
dark clouds of doubt now my path-way ob-scure,
gates of the Cit-y be-yond I can see,
hap-py, so hap-py, as on-ward I go,

since

Refrain

Je-sus came in-to my heart!

Since Je-sus came in-to my
Since Je-sus came in, came

WORDS: R. H. McDaniel
MUSIC: Charles H. Gabriel

McDANIEL
12 8.12 8 with Refrain

heart, since Je - sus came in - to my
in - to my heart, since Je - sus came in, came

heart, floods of joy o'er my soul like the
in - to my heart,

sea bil-lows roll, since Je - sus came in - to my heart.

There's a Song 2141

1. There's a song of *love in my heart; *love is a gift from Je - sus.

There's a song of *love in my heart; *love is a gift from God.

Al - le - lu - ia! *Love in my heart is sing-ing prais-es.

Al - le - lu - ia! *Love is a gift from God.

*2. Peace   3. Faith   4. Hope   5. Joy

WORDS: Handt Hanson
MUSIC: Handt Hanson

HANSON
87.86.49.46

© 1996 Changing Church Forum

Blessed Quietness

1. Joys are flow - ing like a riv - er, since the
2. Bring-ing life and health and glad - ness all a -
3. Like the rain that falls from heav - en, like the
4. See, a fruit - ful field is grow - ing, bless - ed
5. What a won - der - ful sal - va - tion, when we

Com - fort - er has come; Christ a - bides with us for -
round, this heaven - ly Guest ban-ished un - be - lief and
sun - light from the sky, so the Spir - it, too, is
fruit of righ - teous - ness; and the streams of life are
al - ways see Christ's face, what a per - fect hab - i -

ev - er, makes the trust - ing heart a home.
sad - ness, changed our wea - ri - ness to rest.
giv - en, com - ing on us from on high.
flow - ing in the lone - ly wil - der - ness.
ta - tion, what a qui - et rest - ing place.

Refrain

Bless - ed qui - et - ness, ho - ly qui - et - ness, what a s -

WORDS: Manie P. Ferguson (Matt. 8:24-26; John 14:16-19)
MUSIC: W. S. Marshall; arr. by J. Jefferson Cleveland and Verolga Nix

BLESSED QUIETNESS
87.87 with Refrain

sur - ance in my soul. On the storm-y sea, Je-sus speaks to me, and the bil - lows cease to roll.

O Lord, Your Tenderness 2143

O Lord, your ten - der-ness, melt-ing all my bit - ter-ness; O Lord, I re-ceive your love.

O Lord, your love - li - ness, chang-ing my un - worth - i - ness; O Lord, I re-ceive your love.

O Lord, I re-ceive your love; O Lord, I re-ceive your love.

WORDS: Graham Kendrick (Isa. 61:3)
MUSIC: Graham Kendrick

YOUR TENDERNESS
Irregular

2144

Why We Sing
(Someone Asked the Question)

1. Some-one asked the ques - tion, —
   Some-one may be won - dering —
2. When the song is o - ver, —
   if some-bod - y asks you, —
3. When we cross that riv - er to

"Why do we sing? When we
when we sing our song, — at
we've all said, "A - men," in your
"Was it just a show," lift your
stu - dy war no more, we will

lift our hands to Je - sus — what
times we may be cry - ing — and
heart just keep on sing - ing and the
hands and be a wit - ness — and
sing our song to Je - sus, — the

1, 3
do we real - ly mean?" —

song will nev - er end. And

2, 4, 5
noth-ing's real - ly wrong.

tell the whole world, "No!"
One whom we a - dore!

Refrain

I sing be-cause I'm hap - py! I sing be-cause I'm free! God's

eye is on the spar - row — That's the rea-son why I sing.

Glo-ry hal - le - lu - jah! You're the rea-son why I sing.

WORDS: Kirk Franklin (Isa. 2:4; Mic. 4:3)
MUSIC: Kirk Franklin

WHY WE SING
Irregular with Refrain

Glo-ry hal - le-lu - jah! You're the rea-son why I sing.

Glo-ry hal - le-lu - jah! I give the prais-es to you.

Glo-ry hal - le-lu - jah! You're the rea-son why I sing.

I've Got Peace Like a River 2145

1. I've got peace like a riv-er, I've got peace like a

riv - er, I've got peace like a riv - er in my

soul. _____ I've got riv-er in my soul. _____

2. I've got joy like a fountain ...   3. I've got love like an ocean ...

WORDS: African American spiritual
MUSIC: African American spiritual

PEACE LIKE A RIVER
77.11 D

2146 His Eye Is on the Sparrow

1. Why should I feel dis-cour-aged? Why should the shad-ows come? Why should my heart be lone-ly and long for heaven and home, When Je-sus is my por-tion? My con-stant friend is he: His eye is on the spar-row, and I know he watch-es me; his eye is on the spar-row, and I know he watch-es me. I sing be-cause I'm hap-py, (I'm hap-py,) I sing be-cause I'm free, (I'm free,) for his

2. "Let not your heart be trou-bled," his ten-der word I hear, and rest-ing on his good-ness, I lose my doubts and fears; though by the path he lead-eth but one step I may see:

3. When-ev-er I am tempt-ed, when-ev-er clouds a-rise, when song gives place to sigh-ing, when hope with-in me dies, I draw the clo-ser to him, from care he sets me free:

WORDS: Civilla Martin (Luke 12:6-7; John 14:1)
MUSIC: Charles H. Gabriel

SPARROW
Irregular with Refrain

eye is on the spar-row, and I know he watch-es me.

There Are Some Things I May Not Know 2147
(Yes, God Is Real)

1. There are some things I may not know, there are some
2. Some folks may doubt, some folks may scorn, all can de -
3. I can - not tell just how you felt when Je - sus

plac - es I can't go, but I am sure of this one
sert and leave me a - lone, but as for me I'll take God's
took your sins a - way, but since that day, yes, since that

thing, that God is real for I can feel God deep with - in.
part, for God is real and I can feel God in my heart.
hour, God has been real for I can feel God's ho - ly power.

Refrain

Yes, God is real, real in my soul; yes, God is real for God has

washed and made me whole; God's love for me is like pure

gold, yes, God is real for I can feel God in my soul.

WORDS: Kenneth Morris
MUSIC: Kenneth Morris

YES, GOD IS REAL
88.8 12 with Refrain

2148 Over My Head

Refrain

O-ver my head, I hear mu-sic in the air; o-ver my head, I hear mu-sic in the air; o-ver my head, I hear mu-sic in the air; there must be a God some - where.

Fine

Leader

1. Oh, when the world is si - lent, _____ oh,
2. And when I'm feel-ing lone-ly, _____ and
3. Now when I think on Je - sus, _____ now

All

Hmm, I hear mu-sic in the air;

WORDS: African American spiritual
MUSIC: African American spiritual; arr. by John Bell, alt.

MUSIC IN THE AIR
Irregular with Refrain

when the world is si - lent, _____ oh,
when I'm feel-ing lone-ly, _____ and
when I think on Je - sus, _____ now

hmm, I hear mu-sic in the air;

when the world is si - lent, _____
when I'm feel-ing lone-ly, _____
when I think on Je - sus, _____

hmm I hear mu-sic in the air;

D.C.

there must be a God some - where.

D.C.

there must be a God some - where.

PARDON AND ASSURANCE, *see further:*

2149 Living for Jesus

1. Liv - ing for Je - sus a life that is true,
2. Liv - ing for Je - sus who died in my place,
3. Liv - ing for Je - sus wher - ev - er I am,
4. Liv - ing for Je - sus through earth's lit - tle while,

striv - ing to please him in all that I do,
bear - ing on Cal - vary my sin and dis - grace,
do - ing each du - ty in his ho - ly name,
my dear - est trea - sure, the light of his smile,

yield - ing al - le - giance, glad - heart - ed and free,
such love con - strains me to an - swer his call,
will - ing to suf - fer af - flic - tion or loss,
seek - ing the lost ones he died to re - deem,

this is the path - way of bless - ing for me.
fol - low his lead - ing and give him my all.
deem - ing each tri - al a part of my cross.
bring - ing the wea - ry to find rest in him.

WORDS: T. O. Chisolm
MUSIC: C. Harold Lowden

LIVING FOR JESUS
10 10.10 10 with Refrain

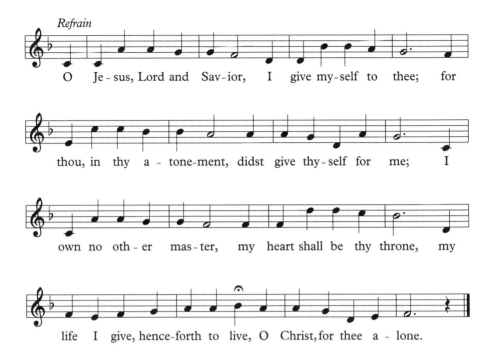

O Je-sus, Lord and Sav-ior, I give my-self to thee; for
thou, in thy a-tone-ment, didst give thy-self for me; I
own no oth-er mas-ter, my heart shall be thy throne, my
life I give, hence-forth to live, O Christ, for thee a-lone.

Lord, Be Glorified 2150

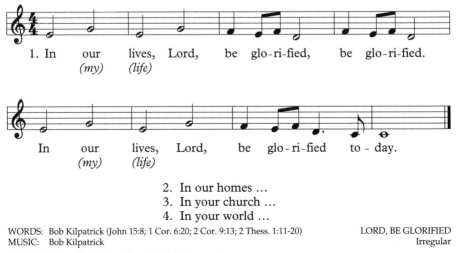

1. In our lives, Lord, be glo-ri-fied, be glo-ri-fied.
   (my) (life)
   In our lives, Lord, be glo-ri-fied to-day.
   (my) (life)

2. In our homes ...
3. In your church ...
4. In your world ...

WORDS: Bob Kilpatrick (John 15:8; 1 Cor. 6:20; 2 Cor. 9:13; 2 Thess. 1:11-20)
MUSIC: Bob Kilpatrick

LORD, BE GLORIFIED
Irregular

2151   I'm So Glad Jesus Lifted Me

1. I'm so glad,
2. Sa-tan had me bound,
3. When I was in trou-ble,
} Je-sus lift-ed me,

I'm so glad,
Sa-tan had me bound,
when I was in trou-ble,
} Je-sus lift-ed me,

I'm so glad,
Sa-tan had me bound,
when I was in trou-ble,
} Je-sus lift-ed me, sing-ing

glo-ry, hal-le-lu-jah, Je-sus lift-ed me.

WORDS: African American spiritual
MUSIC: African American spiritual

I'M SO GLAD
Irregular

Change My Heart, O God

2152

Change my heart, O God, make it ev-er true.

Change my heart, O God,

may I be like you. You are the

Pot - ter, I am the clay.

Mold me and make me, this is what I

pray. Change my heart, O

God, make it ev-er true. Change my heart, O God,

may I be like you.

WORDS: Eddie Espinosa (Isa. 64:8)
MUSIC: Eddie Espinosa

CHANGE MY HEART
Irregular

2153 I'm Gonna Live So God Can Use Me

WORDS: African American spiritual
MUSIC: African American spiritual; arr. by Wendell Whalum

Arr. © Estate of Wendell Whalum

I'M GONNA LIVE
Irregular

Please Enter My Heart, Hosanna 2154

WORDS: Cathy Townley
MUSIC: Cathy Townley

ENTER MY HEART
Irregular

Blest Are They

1. Blest are they, the poor in spir-it; theirs is the
2. Blest are they, the low - ly ones; they shall in -
3. Blest are they who show mer-cy; mer - cy
4. Blest are they who seek peace; they are the
5. Blest are you who suf - fer hate, all be -

king-dom of God. _____ Blest are they,
her - it the earth. _____ Blest are they who
shall be theirs. _____ Blest are they, the
chil-dren of God. _____ Blest are they who
cause of me. _____ Re - joice and be glad,

full of sor - row; they shall be con - soled. _____
hun-ger and thirst; they shall have their fill. _____
pure of heart; they shall see God! _____
suf - fer in faith; the glo - ry of God is theirs. _____
yours is the king-dom. Shine for all to see. _____

Refrain

Re - joice _____ and be glad! _____ Bless-ed are

you, ho - ly are you. Re - joice _____ and be glad! _

_ Yours is the king-dom of God! _____

WORDS: David Haas (Matt. 5:3-16)
MUSIC: David Haas

BLEST ARE THEY
Irregular with Refrain

© 1985 GIA Publications, Inc.

Give Peace
(Da Pacem Cordium)

2156

Give peace to ev-ery heart. Give peace to ev-ery heart. Give
Da pa-cem cor-di-um. Da pa-cem cor-di-um. Da

peace, _____ Lord. Give peace, _____ Lord.
pa - cem. Da pa - cem.

May be sung as a canon. Ⓐ may always be sung by the congregation if desired; soloists or the choir singing Ⓑ and Ⓒ.

WORDS: Anon.
MUSIC: Jacques Berthier and the Community of Taizé

DA PACEM
Irregular

Come and Fill Our Hearts
(Confitemini Domino)

2157

Come and fill our hearts with your peace.
Con - fi - te - mi - ni Do - mi - no

You a-lone, O Lord, are ho - ly. Come and fill our hearts
quo - ni - am bo - nus. Con - fi - te - mi - ni

with your peace, Al - le - lu - ia!
Do - mi - no, Al - le - lu - ia!

WORDS: Jacques Berthier (Ps. 137)
MUSIC: Jacques Berthier

CONFITEMINI DOMINO
Irregular

2158   Just a Closer Walk with Thee

1. I am weak, but thou art strong;
2. Through this world of toil and snares,
3. When my fee-ble life is o'er,

Je - sus, keep me from all wrong;   I'll be sat - is - fied as
if I fal - ter, Lord, who cares?   Who with me my bur-den
time for me will be no more;   guide me gent-ly, safe - ly

long   as I walk, let me walk close to thee.
shares?   None but thee, dear Lord, none but thee.
o'er   to thy shore, dear Lord, to thy shore.

Refrain

Just a clos-er walk with thee,   grant it, Je-sus, is my plea,

dai - ly walk-ing close to thee: Let it be, dear Lord, let it be.

WORDS: Anon. (James 4:8)
MUSIC: Anon.

CLOSER WALK
Irregular with Refrain

2159   Jesus, Draw Me Close

Je-sus, draw me close, _   clos-er, Lord, to you. _

(For)

WORDS: Rick Founds (James 4:8)
MUSIC: Rick Founds

DRAW ME CLOSE
Irregular

Let the world a-round me fade a-way.

I de-sire to wor-ship and o-bey.

Into My Heart

2160

1. In-to my heart, in-to my heart, come
2. Out of my heart, out of my heart, shine

in-to my heart, Lord Je - sus; come in to-day, come
out of my heart, Lord Je - sus; shine out to-day, shine

in to stay; come in-to my heart, Lord Je - sus.
out al-way; shine out of my heart, Lord Je - sus.

WORDS: Harry D. Clarke; st. 2 anon.
MUSIC: Harry D. Clarke

INTO MY HEART
448.448

To Know You More

1. To know you in all of your glo - ry, to
(2., 4. To) know you in all of your pow - er, to
(3. To) know you in all of your mer - cy, to

love you with all that I am. With all of my
trust you with all that I am. With all of my
serve you with all that I am. With all of my

1, 3

heart, Lord, this is my prayer: To know you
heart, Lord,
heart, Lord, this is my prayer: To know you

2, 4

more. 2. To
this is my prayer: To
more. 4. To

Second time to Coda ⊕   D.S. al Coda

know you more. 3. To

⊕ CODA

more. To know you more. _____

WORDS: Joe Horness (Phil. 3:10)
MUSIC: Joe Horness

TO KNOW YOU MORE
98.554

Grace Alone

1. Ev - ery prom - ise we can make, ev - ery prayer and
2. Ev - ery soul we long to reach, ev - ery heart we

step of faith, ev - ery dif-ference we will make
hope to teach, ev - ery-where we share his peace

is on-ly by his grace. Ev - ery moun - tain
is on-ly by his grace. Ev - ery lov - ing

we will climb, ev - ery ray of hope we shine,
word we say, ev - ery tear we wipe a - way,

ev - ery bless - ing left be-hind }
ev - ery sor - row turned to praise } is on-ly by his

Refrain

grace. Grace a - lone which God sup-plies, strength un-

known he will pro-vide. Christ in us our Cor-ner-

stone; we will go forth in grace a - lone.

WORDS: Scott Wesley Brown and Jeff Nelson (Eph. 2:8-10)
MUSIC: Scott Wesley Brown and Jeff Nelson

GRACE ALONE
Irregular with Refrain

© 1998 Maranatha! Music, admin. by The Copyright Co.

2163 He Who Began a Good Work in You

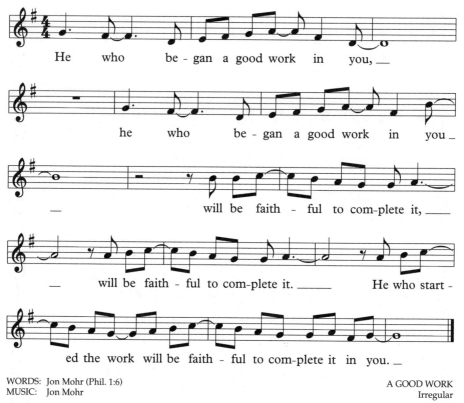

He who be-gan a good work in you, ___

he who be-gan a good work in you ___

___ will be faith-ful to com-plete it, ___

___ will be faith-ful to com-plete it. ___ He who start-

ed the work will be faith-ful to com-plete it in you. ___

WORDS: Jon Mohr (Phil. 1:6)
MUSIC: Jon Mohr

A GOOD WORK
Irregular

© 1987 Jonathan Mark Music and Birdwing Music

2164 Sanctuary

Lord, pre-pare me to be a sanc-tu-ar-y, pure and

ho-ly, tried and true. With thanks-giv-ing, I'll be a

liv-ing sanc-tu-ar-y for you.

WORDS: John Thompson and Randy Scruggs
MUSIC: John Thompson and Randy Scruggs

SANCTUARY
Irregular

© 1982 Whole Armor/Full Armor Music, admin. by The Kruger Organization

Cry of My Heart

Refrain

It is the cry of my heart to fol - low you.

It is the cry of my heart to be close to you.

It is the cry of my heart to fol - low

Fine

all of the days of my life. ___

1. Teach me your ho - ly ways, ___ O Lord, ___
2. O - pen my eyes so I ___ can see the

so I can walk in your truth. ___
won - der - ful things that you do. ___

Teach me your ho - ly ways, ___ O Lord, and make me
O - pen my heart up more ___ and more, and make me

D.C.

whol - ly de - vot - ed to you. ___
whol - ly de - vot - ed to you. ___

WORDS: Terry Butler (Ps. 25:4-5)
MUSIC: Terry Butler

CRY OF MY HEART
Irregular with Refrain

2166 Christ Beside Me

1., 3. Christ be - side me, Christ be - fore me,
2. Christ on my right hand, Christ on my left hand,

Christ be - hind me — King of my heart; _____
Christ all a - round me — shield in the strife; _____

Christ with - in me, Christ be - low me,
Christ in my sleep - ing, Christ in my sit - ting,

Christ a - bove me — nev - er to part. _____
Christ in my ris - ing — light of my life. _____

WORDS: *St. Patrick's Breastplate;* adapt. by James Quinn
MUSIC: Trad. Gaelic melody

BUNESSAN
55.54 D

Adapt. © James Quinn S. J. Used by permission of Selah Publishing Co., Inc.

2167 More Like You

More like you, Je - sus, more like you.

Fill my heart with your de - sire to make me more like you.

More like you, Je - sus, more like you.

Fine

Touch my lips with ho - ly fire and make me more like you.

WORDS: Scott Wesley Brown
MUSIC: Scott Wesley Brown

MORE LIKE YOU
Irregular

© 1997 Maranatha Praise, Inc., admin. by The Copyright Co.

Lord, you are my mer-cy. Lord, you are my grace.

All my deep-est sins have for-ev-er been e-rased.

Draw me in your pres-ence. Lead me in your ways. I

D.C. al Fine

long to bring you glo-ry in right-teous-ness and praise.

Love the Lord Your God 2168

Love the Lord, your God, _____ with all your

heart. _____ Love the Lord, your God, _____ with

all your soul. _____ Love the Lord, your

God, _____ with all your mind. _____ Love the

Lord, your God, _____ with all that you are. _____

WORDS: Jean and Jim Strathdee (Deut. 6:5; Matt. 22:37; Mark 12:30; Luke 10:27)   GREAT COMMANDMENT
MUSIC: Jean and Jim Strathdee   Irregular
© 1991 Desert Flower Music

2169 God, How Can We Forgive

1. God, how can we for-give when bonds of love are torn?
2. When we have missed the mark, and tears of an-guish flow,
3. Who dares to throw the stone to damn an-oth-er's sin,

How can we rise and start a-new, our trust re-born?
how can you still re-lease our guilt, the debt we owe?
when you, while know-ing all our past, for-give a-gain?

When hu-man lov-ing fails and ev-ery hope is gone,
The o-cean depth of grace sur-pass-es all our needs.
No more we play the judge, for by your grace we live.

your love gives strength be-yond our own to face the dawn.
A priest who shares our hu-man pain, Christ in-ter-cedes.
As you, O God, for-give our sin, may we for-give.

WORDS: Ruth Duck (Matt. 6:12-15; 18:21-35; John 8:2-11)
MUSIC: Hebrew melody, *Sacred Harmony;* harm. from *Hymns Ancient and Modern,* alt.

LEONI
66.84 D

God Made from One Blood

2170

1. God made from one blood all the fam-ilies of earth,
2. We turn to you, God, with our thanks and our tears
3. We learn through our fam-ilies how close-ness and trust
4. Give, Lord, to each fam-ily in con-flict and storm
5. Then wid-en that wis-dom and grace to in-clude

the cir-cles of nur-ture that raised us from birth,
for all of the fam-ilies we've known through the years,
in-crease when our ac-tions are lov-ing and just.
a sense of your wis-dom and grace that trans-form
the rac-es and view-points our fam-ilies ex-clude

com-pan-ions who join us to walk through each stage
the in-ti-mate net-works on whom we de-pend
Yet fam-ilies have al-so dis-tort-ed their roles,
sharp an-ger to in-sight which strength-ens the heart
till peace in each home bears and nur-tures the bud

of child-hood and youth and a-dult-hood and age.
of par-ent and part-ner and room-mate and friend.
mis-treat-ing their mem-bers and bruis-ing their souls.
and makes clear the place where re-build-ing can start.
of peace shared by all you have made from one blood.

WORDS: Thomas H. Troeger (Acts 17:26)
MUSIC: Welsh folk melody

ST. DENIO
11 11.11 11

2171 Make Me a Channel of Your Peace

1. Make me a chan-nel of your peace. _____ Where
2. Make me a chan-nel of your peace. _____ Where
4. Make me a chan-nel of your peace. _____ It

there is ha-tred, let me bring your love. _____ Where
there's de-spair in life, let me bring hope. _____ Where
is in par-don-ing that we are par-doned, _____ in

there is in-ju-ry, your par-don, Lord, _____ and
there is dark-ness, _____ on-ly light, _____ and
giv-ing of our-selves that we re-ceive, _____ and in

|1| |2, 4 *Fine*|

where there's doubt, true faith in you. _____
where there's sad-ness, ev-er joy. _____
dy-ing that we're born to e-ter-nal life. _____

3. Oh, Mas-ter, grant that I may nev-er seek _____ so

much to be con-soled as to con-sole, _____ to be

un-der-stood as to un-der-stand, _____ to be

D.C.

loved as to love with all my soul. _____

WORDS: *Prayer of St. Francis;* adapt. by Sebastian Temple (Matt. 6:12-15)
MUSIC: Sebastian Temple

CHANNEL OF PEACE
Irregular

We Are Called

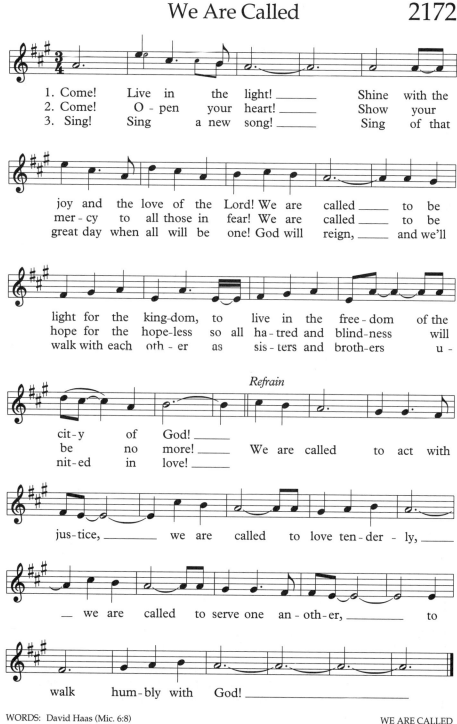

1. Come! Live in the light! _____ Shine with the
2. Come! O-pen your heart! _____ Show your
3. Sing! Sing a new song! _____ Sing of that

joy and the love of the Lord! We are called _____ to be
mer-cy to all those in fear! We are called _____ to be
great day when all will be one! God will reign, _____ and we'll

light for the king-dom, to live in the free-dom of the
hope for the hope-less so all ha-tred and blind-ness will
walk with each oth-er as sis-ters and broth-ers u-

Refrain

cit-y of God! _____ We are called to act with
be no more! _____
nit-ed in love! _____

jus-tice, _____ we are called to love ten-der-ly, _____

_____ we are called to serve one an-oth-er, _____ to

walk hum-bly with God! _____

WORDS: David Haas (Mic. 6:8)
MUSIC: David Haas

© 1988 GIA Publications, Inc.

WE ARE CALLED
Irregular with Refrain

2173 Shine, Jesus, Shine

Refrain

Shine, Je-sus, shine, _ fill this land with the Fa-ther's glo-ry,
blaze, Spir-it, blaze, _ set our hearts on fire;
flow, riv-er, flow, _ flood the na-tions with grace and mer-cy,

Fine

send forth your word, _ Lord, and let there be light.

1. Lord, the light of your love is shin-ing
2. Lord, I come to your awe-some pres-ence
3. As we gaze on your king-ly bright-ness,

in the midst of the dark-ness shin-ing;
from the shad-ows in-to your ra-di-ance;
so our fac-es dis-play your like-ness;

Je-sus, Light of the World, shine up-on us,
by the blood I may en-ter your bright-ness,
ev-er chang-ing from glo-ry to glo-ry,

set us free by the truth you now bring us.
search me, try me, con-sume all my dark-ness.
mir-rored here may our lives tell your sto-ry.

WORDS: Graham Kendrick (2 Cor. 4:6)
MUSIC: Graham Kendrick

SHINE, JESUS, SHINE
Irregular with Refrain

D.C.

Shine on me, shine on me.
Shine on me, shine on me.
Shine on me, shine on me.

What Does the Lord Require of You 2174

1. *(Basses)*

What does the Lord re-quire of you?

2. *(Altos and Tenors in unison)**

Jus - tice, kind - ness,

3. *(Sopranos)***

To seek jus-tice and love kind-ness

Repeat as desired.

| Repeat ending | Last |

What does the Lord re-quire of you? you?

walk hum-bly with your God. God.

and walk hum-bly with your God. God.

*Enter on first repeat.
**Enter on second repeat.

WORDS: Jim Strathdee (Mic. 6:8)
MUSIC: Jim Strathdee

MOON
Irregular

© 1986 Desert Flower Music

2175 Together We Serve

1. To - geth - er we serve, u - nit - ed by love, in -
2. We seek to be - come a bea - con of hope, a
3. We wel-come the scarred, the wealth - y, the poor, the
4. To - geth - er, by grace, we wit - ness and work, re -

vit - ing God's world to the glo - ri - ous feast. We
lamp for the heart and a light for the feet. We
bus - y, the lone - ly, and all who need care. We
mem - ber - ing Je - sus, in whom we grow strong. To -

work and we pray through sor - row and joy, ex -
learn, year by year, to let love shine through un -
of - fer a home to those who will come, our
geth - er we serve in Spir - it and truth, re -

tend - ing your love to the last and the least.
til we see Christ in each per - son we meet.
hands quick to help, our hearts read - y to dare.
mem - ber - ing love is the strength of our song.

WORDS: Daniel Charles Damon
MUSIC: Daniel Charles Damon
SAN ANSELMO
55.11 D

© 1998 Hope Publishing Co.

2176 Make Me a Servant

Make me a ser-vant, hum-ble and meek, Lord, let me

lift up those who are weak. And may the prayer of my

heart al - ways be: Make me a ser-vant, make me a

WORDS: Kelly Willard (John 13:14-16)
MUSIC: Kelly Willard
MAKE ME A SERVANT
Irregular

© 1982 Willing Heart Music, admin. by Maranatha! Music c/o The Copyright Co.

ser - vant, make me a ser - vant to - day. _____

Wounded World that Cries for Healing 2177

1. Wound - ed world that cries for heal - ing —
2. Through our na - tion's spent frus - tra - tion,
3. Hon - or those whose lov - ing spir - it

here we hold each oth - er's pain, wound - ed sys - tems,
through the cor - ri - dors of stress may there move a
nurs - es hope, re - stores and heals, towel and ba - sin

bruised and bleed - ing bear the load, the scars of strain;
kind - lier wis - dom all may feel, and all may bless;
used in ser - vice like the Christ who comes and kneels;

dol - lars ra - tion out com - pas - sion,
tax and tithe are for a pur - pose
in the tend - ing, in the mend - ing

hard de - ci - sions rule the day, Je - sus of the
shared to shield the poor and weak; past the symp - toms
may we see the right and fair, in our com - mon

heal - ing Spir - it, free us to an - oth - er way!
of our sick - ness let the voice of jus - tice speak.
quest for whole - ness heal each oth - er by our care.

WORDS: Shirley Erena Murray
MUSIC: Hal H. Hopson

HEALING SPIRIT
87.87 D

© 1996 Hope Publishing Co.

2178 Here Am I

1. Here am I, where un-der-neath the brid-ges
2. Here am I, with peo-ple in the line-up,
3. Here am I, where two or three are gath-ered,

in our win-ter cit-ies home-less peo-ple sleep. Here am I, where
anx-ious for a hand-out, ach-ing for a job. Here am I, when
read-y to be al-tered, shar-ing wine and bread. Here am I, where

in de-cay-ing hous-es lit-tle chil-dren shiv-er,
pen-sion-ers and strik-ers sing and march to-geth-er,
those who hear the preach-ing change their way of liv-ing,

cry-ing at the cold. Where are you?
want-ing some-thing new. Where are you?
find the way to life. Where are you?

WORDS: Brian Wren (Matt. 25:31-46)
MUSIC: Daniel Charles Damon

STANISLAUS
37.65 D 3

2179 Live in Charity
(Ubi Caritas)

Live in char-i-ty and stead-fast love,
U - bi ca-ri-tas et a - mor,

Stanzas included in other editions.

WORDS: 9th cent. Latin (1 Cor. 13:2-8)
MUSIC: Jacques Berthier and the Community of Taizé

UBI CARITAS (TAIZÉ)
Irregular

live   in   char - i - ty;   God will   dwell   with   you.
u - bi   ca - ri - tas   De - us   i - bi   est.

Why Stand So Far Away, My God?   2180

1. Why   stand   so   far   a - way,   my   God? Why
2. Why   do   you   hide   when,   full   of   lies,   they
3. The   weak   are crushed   and   fall   to   earth;   the
4. In   a - ges   past   you   heard   the   voice   of
5. A - rise,   O   God,   and   lift   your   hand; bring

hide   in   times   of   need?   The   proud,   un - bri - dled,
mur - der   and   be - tray?   They   wait   to   pounce up -
wick - ed   strut   and   preen.   Why   in   these cruel, cha -
those   the proud   op - press.   Re - mem - ber   those who
jus - tice   to   the   poor.   Come,   help   us   stop   the

chase   the   poor,   and   curse   you   in   their   greed.
on   the   weak   as   li - ons   stalk   their   prey.
o - tic   times   can - not   your   face   be   seen?
suf - fer   now, who   cry   in   deep   dis - tress.
flow   of   blood! Let   ter - ror   reign   no   more!

WORDS: Ruth Duck (Ps. 10)   MORNING SONG
MUSIC: Wyeth's *Repository of Sacred Music, Part Second*   CM
Words © 1992 GIA Publications, Inc.

2181 — We Need a Faith

1. We need a faith so col-or-blind, so
2. We need an eth-ic of re-spect, an
3. We need to act as well as speak, to
4. Come, Chris-tians, look for char-ac-ter and

free from time-worn lies, that when we look from
hon-est pledge of trust, that when we share the
see each oth-er's sweat, that as we la-bor
not for shade of skin, that as we rend the

face to face we see the eyes of God.
deep-est things we feel the warmth of God.
side by side we do the work of God.
walls of race we live the peace of God.

WORDS: John Thornburg
MUSIC: Jesse Seymour Irvine

CRIMOND
CM

Words © 1995 Abingdon Press, admin. by The Copyright Co.

2182 When God Restored Our Common Life

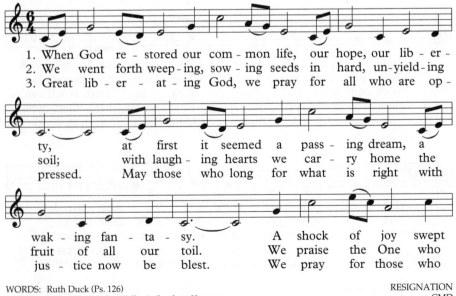

1. When God re-stored our com-mon life, our hope, our lib-er-
2. We went forth weep-ing, sow-ing seeds in hard, un-yield-ing
3. Great lib-er-at-ing God, we pray for all who are op-

ty, at first it seemed a pass-ing dream, a
soil; with laugh-ing hearts we car-ry home the
pressed. May those who long for what is right with

wak-ing fan-ta-sy. A shock of joy swept
fruit of all our toil. We praise the One who
jus-tice now be blest. We pray for those who

WORDS: Ruth Duck (Ps. 126)
MUSIC: USA folk melody, Walker's *Southern Harmony*

RESIGNATION
CMD

Words © 1992 GIA Publications, Inc.

o - ver us, for we had wept so long; the
gave the growth, with voic - es full and strong. The
mourn this day, and all who suf - fer wrong; may

seeds we wa-tered once with tears sprang up in-to a song.
seeds we wa-tered once with tears sprang up in-to a song.
seeds they wa - ter now with tears spring up in-to a song.

Unsettled World   2183

1. Un - set - tled world, where peo - ple long to
2. Un - set - tled world, where mon - ey rules and
3. Un - set - tled world, where an - gry poor from
4. Un - set - tled world, un - set - tled church, whose

find their way, to feel se - cure, from lives of tur - bu -
greed - y sys - tems call the tune; for strength to keep our
grind - ing need at af-fluence stare, with tears and thirst for
struc-tures creak and doc-trines swirl, by faith, and in the

lence and rush we come, to seek your peace, our
val - ues straight we come, with trust in you, O
truth and right we come, with long - ing in our
strength of Christ, we strive, in true com - mu - ni -

God, your word to hear, our faith to live.
God, your word to hear, our faith to live.
hearts, your word to hear, our faith to live.
ty, your word to hear, our faith to live.

WORDS: David Sparks
MUSIC: Hal H. Hopson

THUNDER BAY
88.888

© 1994 Hope Publishing Co.

2184 Sent Out in Jesus' Name

(Enviado Soy de Dios)

Sent out in Je-sus' name, our hands are rea-dy now to
En - via-do soy de Dios, mi ma - no lis-ta es - tá pa - ra

make the earth the place in which the king-dom comes.
cons - tru - ir con El un mun - do fra - ter - nal.

The an-gels can-not change a world of hurt and pain in -
Los án - ge - les no son en - via-dos a cam - biar un

to a world of love, of jus-tice and of peace. The
mun-do de do - lor por un mun-do de paz. Me

task is ours to do, to set it real-ly free. O
ha to - ca-do a mí ha - cer - lo rea - li - dad; a -

help us to o - bey and car - ry out your will.
yú - da - me, Se - ñor, a ha - cer tu vo - lun - tad.

WORDS: Anon.; trans. by Jorge Maldonado, alt.
MUSIC: Trad. Cuban; arr. by Carmen Peña

ENVIADO
12 12.12 12 D

2185 For One Great Peace

1. This thread I weave, this step I dance, this
2. this pot I shape, this fire I light, this
3. this check I write, this march I join, this

WORDS: Shirley Erena Murray
MUSIC: Jim Strathdee

POXON
LM

stone I carve, this ball I bounce, this nail I drive, this
fence I leap, this bone I knit, this seed I nurse, this
faith I state, this truth I sign, this is small part, in

pearl I string, this flag I wave, this note I sing,
rift I mend, this child I raise, this earth I tend,
one small place, of one heart's beat for one great Peace.

Song of Hope
(Canto de Esperanza)
2186

May the God of hope go with us ev - ery day, _ fill-ing all our
¡Dios de la es-pe - ran-za, da-nos go - zo y paz! _ Al mun-do en

lives with love and joy and peace. _ May the God of jus-tice speed us
cri - sis, ha - bla tu ver-dad. __ Dios de la jus - ti - cia, mán-da -

on our way, _ bring-ing light and hope to ev-ery land and race. _
nos tu luz, _ luz y es - pe - ran-za en la os-cu - ri - dad. _

Refrain

— Pray - ing, let us work for peace; _ sing - ing,
— O - re - mos por la paz, ___ can - te -

share our joy with all; ___ work - ing for a
mos de tu a-mor. ___ Lu - che - mos

world that's new, _ faith - ful when we hear Christ's call. _
por la paz, _ fie - les a ti, Se - ñor. _

WORDS: Alvin Schutmaat
MUSIC: Argentine folk melody

ARGENTINA
Irregular with Refrain

2187   Now It Is Evening

1. Now it is eve - ning: Lights of the cit - y bid us re -
2. Now it is eve - ning: Lit - tle ones sleep - ing bid us re -
3. Now it is eve - ning: Food on the ta - ble bids us re -
4. Now it is eve - ning: Here in our meet - ing may we re -

mem - ber Christ is our light. Man - y are lone - ly, who will be
mem - ber Christ is our peace. Some are ne - glect - ed, who will be
mem - ber Christ is our life. Man - y are hun - gry, who will be
mem - ber Christ is our friend. Some may be strang-ers, who will be

neigh-bor? Where there is car - ing Christ is our light.
neigh-bor? Where there is car - ing Christ is our peace.
neigh-bor? Where there is shar - ing Christ is our life.
neigh-bor? Where there's a wel - come Christ is our friend.

WORDS: Fred Pratt Green (John 8:12; 14:6, 27; 15:15)
MUSIC: David Haas

EVENING HYMN
55.54 D

Words © 1974 Hope Publishing Co.; music © 1985 GIA Publications, Inc.

2188   The Family Prayer Song

1. Come and fill our homes with your pres - ence;
2. Lord we vow to live ho - ly,

you a - lone are wor - thy of our rev - erence.
bow - ing our knees to you on - ly.

Refrain

As for me and my house, we will serve the Lord. As for

WORDS: Morris Chapman (Josh. 24:15)
MUSIC: Morris Chapman

FAMILY PRAYER
Irregular with Refrain

© 1994 Maranatha Praise, Inc., admin. by The Copyright Co.

me and my house, we will serve the Lord. As for me and my house,

we will serve the Lord. We will serve the Lord.

A Mother Lined a Basket 2189

1. A moth-er lined a bas-ket to keep her ba-by dry,
2. A moth-er sewed a jack-et lined in the soft-est wool,
3. A moth-er laid her ba-by in man-ger lined with straw;
4. Like Joch-e-bed and Han-nah, and Ma-ry, too, we know

then rocked him on a riv-er, lest he a-wake and cry.
then dressed her lit-tle boy-child, her cup of bless-ing full.
then, in the shep-herd's sto-ry, his call from God fore-saw.
the hard-est part of lov-ing is learn-ing to let go.

She let a prin-cess name him her son that he might live.
She brought him to the tem-ple where he would serve and live.
She nur-tured him and taught him the way that he must live.
So when we send our chil-dren out in the world to live,

God's peo-ple had a lead-er. She had such hope to give.
God's peo-ple had a proph-et. She had such faith to give.
God's peo-ple had a sav-ior. She had such love to give.
grant us such hope and faith, God, and love e-nough to give.

WORDS: Mary Nelson Keithahn (Exod. 2:1-10; 6:20; 1 Sam. 1; Luke 2)
MUSIC: John D. Horman

WEST MAIN
76.76 D

2190 Bring Forth the Kingdom

Leader

All

1. You are salt for the earth, O peo-ple: Salt for the
2. You are a light on the hill, O peo-ple: Light for the
3. You are a seed of the Word, O peo-ple: Bring forth the
4. We are a blest and a pil-grim peo-ple: Bound for the

Leader

King-dom of God! Share the fla-vor of
Cit-y of God! Shine so ho-ly and
King-dom of God! Seeds of mer-cy and
King-dom of God! Love our jour-ney and

All

life, O peo-ple: Life in the King-dom of God!
bright, O peo-ple: Shine for the King-dom of God!
seeds of jus-tice, grow in the King-dom of God!
love our home-land: Love is the King-dom of God!

Refrain

Bring forth the King-dom of mer-cy, bring forth the

King-dom of peace; bring forth the King-dom of jus-tice,

bring forth the Cit-y of God! _____

WORDS: Marty Haugen (Matt. 5:13-16)
MUSIC: Marty Haugen

BRING FORTH THE KINGDOM
Irregular with Refrain

© 1986 GIA Publications, Inc.

SOCIAL HOLINESS, *see further:*

Eternal Father, Strong to Save

2191

1. E - ter - nal Fa - ther, strong to save, whose arm has bound the
2. O Sav - ior, whose al - might - y word the wind and waves sub -
3. O Ho - ly Spir - it, who did brood up - on the cha - os
4. O Trin - i - ty of love and power, all trav - elers guard in

rest - less wave, who bid the might - y o - cean deep its
mis - sive heard, who walked up - on the foam - ing deep, and
wild and rude, and bid its an - gry tu - mult cease, and
dan - ger's hour; from rock and tem - pest, fire and foe, pro -

own ap - point - ed lim - its keep: O hear us when we
calm a - mid its rage did sleep: O hear us when we
gave, for fierce con - fu - sion, peace: O hear us when we
tect them where - so - e'er they go; thus ev - er - more shall

cry to thee for those in per - il on the sea.
cry to thee for those in per - il on the sea.
cry to thee for those in per - il on the sea.
rise to thee glad praise from air and land and sea.

WORDS: William Whiting (Gen. 1:2; Job 38:8-11; Matt. 8:23-27; Mark 4:35-41; Luke 8:22-35)
MUSIC: John B. Dykes

MELITA
88.88.88

2192

Freedom Is Coming

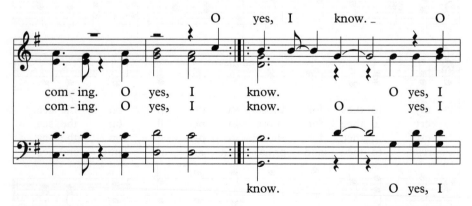

WORDS: Trad. South African
MUSIC: Trad. South African

FREEDOM IS COMING
Irregular

Lord, Listen to Your Children Praying 2193

Lord, lis-ten to your chil-dren pray - ing, _____

Lord, send your Spir-it in this place; _____

Lord, lis-ten to your chil-dren pray - ing, _____ send us

love, send us power, send us grace. _____

WORDS: Ken Medema
MUSIC: Ken Medema

CHILDREN PRAYING
98.99

© 1973 Hope Publishing Co.

2194
O Freedom

1. O   free - dom!   O
2. No   more moan-ing,   no   more
3. No   more weep-ing,   no   more
4. There'll be sing - ing,   there'll be
5. There'll be shout-ing,   there'll be
6. There'll be pray - ing,   there'll be

free - dom!
moan - ing,
weep - ing,
sing - ing,
shout - ing,
pray - ing,

free - dom!   O   free-dom o - ver me. _____
moan-ing,   no   more moan-ing o - ver me. _____
weep-ing,   no   more weep-ing o - ver me. _____
sing - ing,   there'll be sing - ing o - ver me. _____
shout-ing,   there'll be shout-ing o - ver me. _____
pray - ing,   there'll be pray - ing o - ver me. _____

free - dom!
moan - ing,
weep - ing,
sing - ing,
shout - ing,
pray - ing,

Refrain

And   be - fore   I'll   be   a   slave,   I'd   be

WORDS: African American spiritual
MUSIC: African American spiritual; arr. by John Bell

O FREEDOM
Irregular with Refrain

bur - ied in my grave, and go home to my

1-5

6

Lord and be free. (O free - dom.) free.

In the Lord I'll Be Ever Thankful 2195

In the Lord I'll be ev - er thank - ful, in the Lord I will re -

joice! Look to God, do not be a - fraid. Lift up your

voic - es, the Lord is near, lift up your voic - es, the Lord is near.

WORDS: Jacques Berthier

MUSIC: Jacques Berthier

ITLIBET

Irregular

2196 We Walk by Faith

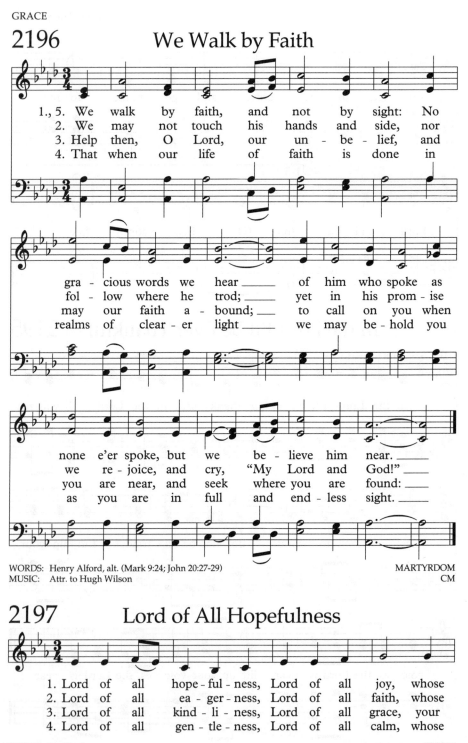

1., 5. We walk by faith, and not by sight: No
2. We may not touch his hands and side, nor
3. Help then, O Lord, our un - be - lief, and
4. That when our life of faith is done in

gra - cious words we hear _____ of him who spoke as
fol - low where he trod; _____ yet in his prom - ise
may our faith a - bound; _____ to call on you when
realms of clear - er light _____ we may be - hold you

none e'er spoke, but we be - lieve him near. _____
we re - joice, and cry, "My Lord and God!" _____
you are near, and seek where you are found: _____
as you are in full and end - less sight. _____

WORDS: Henry Alford, alt. (Mark 9:24; John 20:27-29)   MARTYRDOM
MUSIC: Attr. to Hugh Wilson   CM

2197 Lord of All Hopefulness

1. Lord of all hope - ful - ness, Lord of all joy, whose
2. Lord of all ea - ger - ness, Lord of all faith, whose
3. Lord of all kind - li - ness, Lord of all grace, your
4. Lord of all gen - tle - ness, Lord of all calm, whose

WORDS: Jan Struther   SLANE
MUSIC: Irish folk melody   10 11.11 12
Words by permission of Oxford University Press

trust, ev - er child - like, no cares could de - stroy: Be
strong hands were skilled at the plane and the lathe: Be
hands swift to wel - come, your arms to em - brace: Be
voice is con - tent-ment, whose pres - ence is balm: Be

there at our wak - ing, and give us, we pray, your
there at our la - bors, and give us, we pray, your
there at our hom - ing, and give us, we pray, your
there at our sleep - ing, and give us, we pray, your

bliss in our hearts, Lord, at the break of the day.
strength in our hearts, Lord, at the noon of the day.
love in our hearts, Lord, at the eve of the day.
peace in our hearts, Lord, at the end of the day.

Stay with Me
(Noho Pū)
2198

Stay with me, re - main here with me, watch and
No - ho pū no - ho mai me ia'u ki - a'i a

pray, watch and pray.
pu - le kiai a pule.

WORDS: Jacques Berthier (Matt. 26); Hawaiian trans.
  by Malcolm Naea Chun (Matt. 26:41; Mark 14:38)
MUSIC: Jacques Berthier

STAY WITH ME
Irregular

© 1984 Les Presses de Taizé (France), admin. by GIA Publications, Inc.

2199 Stay with Us

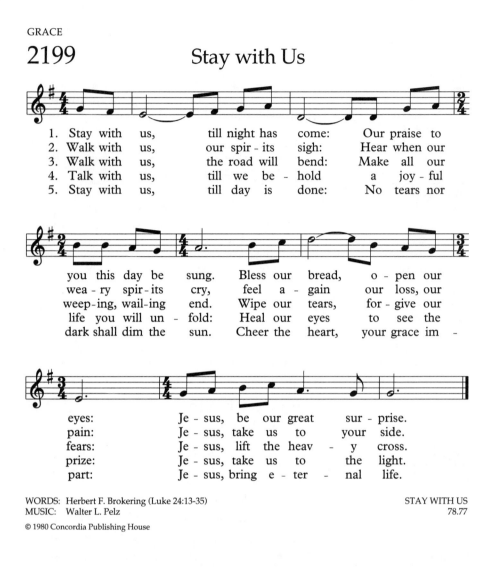

1. Stay with us, till night has come: Our praise to
2. Walk with us, our spir-its sigh: Hear when our
3. Walk with us, the road will bend: Make all our
4. Talk with us, till we be-hold a joy-ful
5. Stay with us, till day is done: No tears nor

you this day be sung. Bless our bread, o-pen our
wea-ry spir-its cry, feel a-gain our loss, our
weep-ing, wail-ing end. Wipe our tears, for-give our
life you will un-fold: Heal our eyes to see the
dark shall dim the sun. Cheer the heart, your grace im -

eyes: Je-sus, be our great sur-prise.
pain: Je-sus, take us to your side.
fears: Je-sus, lift the heav-y cross.
prize: Je-sus, take us to the light.
part: Je-sus, bring e-ter-nal life.

WORDS: Herbert F. Brokering (Luke 24:13-35)
MUSIC: Walter L. Pelz

STAY WITH US
78.77

2200 O Lord, Hear My Prayer

O Lord, hear my prayer. O Lord, hear my prayer.

WORDS: Jacques Berthier (Ps. 102:1-2)
MUSIC: Jacques Berthier

HEAR MY PRAYER
Irregular

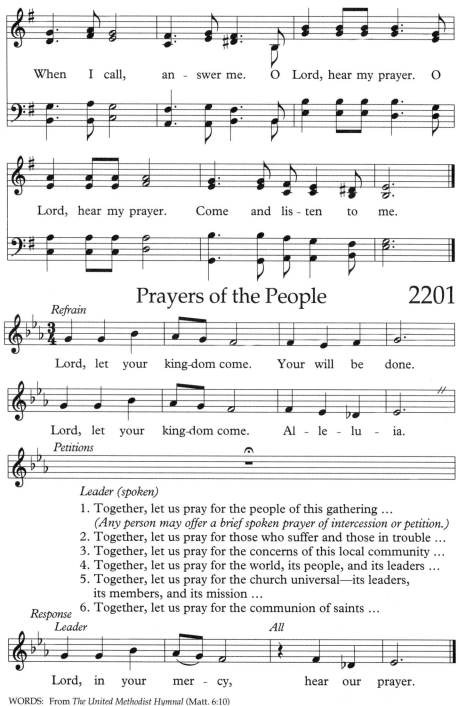

Prayers of the People 2201

Refrain

Lord, let your king-dom come. Your will be done.

Lord, let your king-dom come. Al - le - lu - ia.

Petitions

Leader (spoken)

1. Together, let us pray for the people of this gathering ...
   (Any person may offer a brief spoken prayer of intercession or petition.)
2. Together, let us pray for those who suffer and those in trouble ...
3. Together, let us pray for the concerns of this local community ...
4. Together, let us pray for the world, its people, and its leaders ...
5. Together, let us pray for the church universal—its leaders,
   its members, and its mission ...
6. Together, let us pray for the communion of saints ...

Response

Leader   *All*

Lord, in your mer - cy, hear our prayer.

WORDS: From *The United Methodist Hymnal* (Matt. 6:10)
MUSIC: Bonnie Johansen-Werner

2202 Come Away with Me

1. Come a - way with me to a qui - et
2. Come and pray with me on a gen - tle
3. Come to - day with thoughts of the count - less
4. Come and say, in words whis - pered from your
5. Come a - way with me to a qui - et

place, a - part from the world with its fran - tic
sea, on top of a hill in the Gal - i -
ways that God's stead - fast love bless - es all our
soul, the feel - ings and ac - tions you can't con -
place, to God's lov - ing arms wait - ing to em -

pace, to pray, re - flect, and seek God's grace.
lee, in gar - dens like Geth - se - ma - ne.
days, and join with me in si - lent praise.
trol. Your spir - it needs to be made whole.
brace all those who come in hope of grace.

Come a - way with me. Come a - way.

WORDS: Mary Nelson Keithahn
MUSIC: John D. Horman

RECREATION
10 10.88

© 1997 Abingdon Press, admin. by The Copyright Co.

2203 In His Time

1. In his time, _____ in his time; _____ he makes
2. In your time, _____ in your time; _____ you make

all things beau - ti - ful in his time. _____ Lord, please
all things beau - ti - ful in your time. _____ Lord, my

WORDS: Diane Ball (Eccles. 3:11)
MUSIC: Diane Ball

GOD'S TIME
Irregular

© 1978 Maranatha! Music, admin. by The Copyright Co.

show me ev-ery day as you're teach-ing me your way, that you
life to you I bring; may each song I have to sing be to

do just what you say in your time. ____
you a love-ly thing in your time. ____

Light of the World 2204

1. You are the Light of the World, _ O Lord, and
2. You are the Bread of Life, ___ O Lord, —
3. You've o-ver-come the world, _ O Lord, and

you make your ser - vant shine. _ So
bro-ken to set us free. ___ So
giv-en us vic - to - ry. ___ So

how could there be an - y dark-ness in me if
how could there be an - y hun-ger in me if
why could I fear _ when trou-ble is near if

you are the Light of the World? _____
you are the Bread of Life? _____
you've o - ver - come the world? _____

You are the Light of the World. __
You are the Bread of Life. ___
You've o - ver - come the world. __

WORDS: Michael Card (John 6:35, 48; 9:5; 16:33)
MUSIC: Michael Card
© 1992 Mole End Music, admin. by Word Music, Inc.

LIGHT OF THE WORLD (CARD)
Irregular

2205   The Fragrance of Christ

Refrain

Lord, may our prayer rise like in-cense in your
sight, may this place be filled with the
fra-grance of Christ. _____

1. I will thank you, Lord, with all of my
2. I will thank you, Lord, for your faith-ful-ness and
3. All who live on earth shall give you

heart, you have heard the words of my mouth. ____
love, be-yond all my hopes and dreams. ____
thanks when they hear the words of your voice. ____

— In the pres-ence of the Lord I will
— On the day that I called you
— And all shall sing of your

bless you, _____ I will a-dore be-
an-swered; ____ you gave life to the
ways: _____ "How great is the

fore your ho-ly tem - ple. _____
strength of my soul. _____
glo - ry of God!" _____

WORDS: David Haas (Ps. 138:1-5; 141:2)
MUSIC: David Haas

INCENSE
Irregular with Refrain

Without Seeing You

2206

Refrain

With-out see-ing you, we love you; with-out touch-ing you, we em-brace; with-out know-ing you, we fol-low; with-out see-ing you, _____ we be-lieve. _____

Fine

1. We re-turn to you deep with-in, leave the past to the dust; turn to you with tears and fast-ing; you are read-y to for-give. _____
2. The spar-row will find a home, near to you, O God; how hap-py, we who dwell with you, for-ev-er in your house. _____
3. For-ev-er we sing to you of your good-ness, O God; pro-claim-ing to all the world of your faith-ful-ness and love. _____
4. For you are our shep-herd, there is noth-ing that we need; in green pas-tures we will find our rest, near the wat-ers of peace. _____

D.C.

WORDS: David Haas (Ps. 23:1-2; 1 Pet. 1:8)
MUSIC: David Haas

WE BELIEVE
Irregular with Refrain

2207 Lord, Listen to Your Children

On bend-ed knee with need-y hearts we come and pray. ___ Lord, lis-ten to your chil - dren. ___ With will-ing hearts and o-pen arms we come and pray. ___ Lord, lis - ten to your chil - dren. ___ With sim-ple words of heart-felt thanks we come. Be liev-ing in your prom-is - es, we come. On

Last time to Coda

D.S. al Coda

CODA

chil - dren, lis-ten to your chil - dren.

WORDS: Handt Hanson and Paul Murakami
MUSIC: Handt Hanson and Paul Murakami

LISTEN
Irregular

© 1991 Changing Church Forum

PRAYER, TRUST, HOPE, *see further:*

Guide My Feet

1. Guide my feet while I run this race.

Yes, my Lord!

Guide my feet while I run this race.

Yes, my Lord!

Guide my feet while I run this race, for I

don't want to run this race in vain! (race in vain)

2. Hold my hand ...
3. Stand by me ...
4. I'm your child ...
5. Search my heart ...
6. Guide my feet ...

WORDS: African American spiritual
MUSIC: African American spiritual; harm. by Wendell Whalum

Harm. © Estate of Wendell Whalum

GUIDE MY FEET
88.8 10

2209 How Long, O Lord

1. How long, O Lord,   will you for - get
2. How long, O Lord,   will you for - sake
3. How long, O Lord?   But you for - give

an an - swer to my prayer?
and leave me in this way?
with mer - cy from a - bove.

No to - kens of your love I see, your face is turned a -
When will you come to my re - lief? My heart is o - ver -
I find that all your ways are just; I learn to praise you

way from me; I wres - tle with de - spair!
whelmed with grief, by e - vil night and day!
and to trust in your un - fail - ing love!

WORDS: Barbara Woollett (Ps. 13)   HOW LONG
MUSIC: Christopher Norton   86.886

2210 Joy Comes with the Dawn

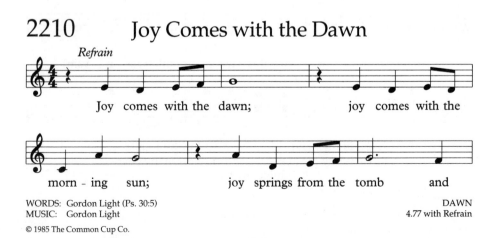

Refrain

Joy comes with the dawn; joy comes with the

morn - ing sun; joy springs from the tomb and

WORDS: Gordon Light (Ps. 30:5)   DAWN
MUSIC: Gordon Light   4.77 with Refrain

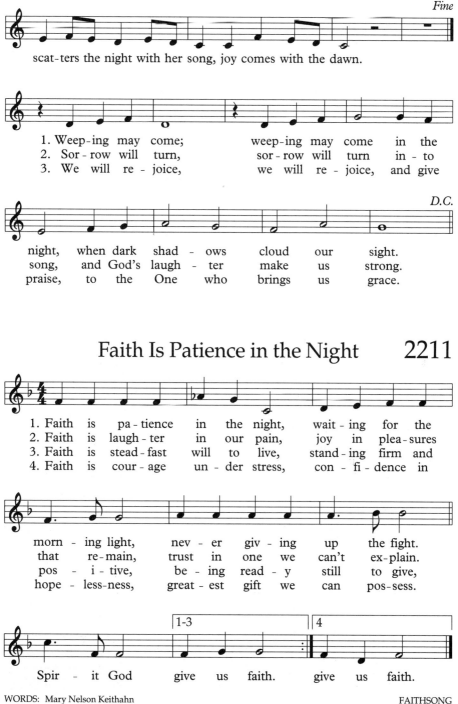

Fine

scat-ters the night with her song, joy comes with the dawn.

1. Weep-ing may come; weep-ing may come in the
2. Sor - row will turn, sor - row will turn in - to
3. We will re - joice, we will re - joice, and give

D.C.

night, when dark shad - ows cloud our sight.
song, and God's laugh - ter make us strong.
praise, to the One who brings us grace.

Faith Is Patience in the Night 2211

1. Faith is pa - tience in the night, wait - ing for the
2. Faith is laugh - ter in our pain, joy in plea - sures
3. Faith is stead - fast will to live, stand - ing firm and
4. Faith is cour - age un - der stress, con - fi - dence in

morn - ing light, nev - er giv - ing up the fight.
that re - main, trust in one we can't ex - plain.
pos - i - tive, be - ing read - y still to give,
hope - less-ness, great - est gift we can pos - sess.

| 1-3 | 4 |

Spir - it God give us faith. give us faith.

WORDS: Mary Nelson Keithahn
MUSIC: John D. Horman

FAITHSONG
77.76

2212 My Life Flows On
(How Can I Keep from Singing)

1. My life flows on in end-less song, a-bove earth's la-men-
2. Through all the tu-mult and the strife, I hear that mu-sic
3. What though my joys and com-forts die? I know my Sav-ior
4. The peace of Christ makes fresh my heart, a foun-tain ev-er

ta - tion. I hear the clear, though far - off hymn that
ring - ing. It finds an ech - o in my soul. How
liv - eth. What though the dark - ness gath - er round? Songs
spring-ing! All things are mine since I am his! How

Refrain

hails a new cre-a-tion.
can I keep from sing-ing?
in the night he giv-eth.   No   storm can shake my
can I keep from sing-ing?

in-most calm   while   to that Rock   I'm   cling-ing. Since

WORDS: Robert Lowry
MUSIC: Robert Lowry

HOW CAN I KEEP FROM SINGING
87.87 with Refrain

love is Lord of heaven and earth, how can I keep from sing-ing?

Healer of Our Every Ill 2213

Refrain

Heal-er of our ev - ery ill, light of each to - mor - row,

Fine

give us peace be-yond our fear, and hope be-yond our sor - row.

1. You who know our fears and sad - ness, grace us with your
2. In the pain and joy be - hold - ing how your grace is
3. Give us strength to love each oth - er, ev - ery sis - ter,
4. You who know each thought and feel - ing, teach us all your

peace and glad - ness; Spir - it of all com - fort,
still un - fold - ing, give us all your vi - sion,
ev - ery broth - er; Spir - it of all kind - ness,
way of heal - ing; Spir - it of com-pas - sion,

D.C.

fill our hearts. _____
God of love. _____
be our guide. _____
fill each heart. _____

WORDS: Marty Haugen
MUSIC: Marty Haugen

© 1987 GIA Publications, Inc.

HEALER OF OUR EVERY ILL
88.63 with Refrain

2214

Lead Me, Guide Me

Lead me, guide me, a-long the way,

for if you lead me, I can-not stray.

Lord, let me walk each day with thee.

Lead me, O Lord, lead me. ____

Stanzas included in other editions.

WORDS: Doris Akers
MUSIC: Doris Akers

© 1953 Doris Akers, renewed, admin. by Unichappell Music, Inc.

LEAD ME, GUIDE ME
Irregular

2215

Cares Chorus

I cast all my cares up-on you, ____ I

lay all of my bur-dens down at your feet, and

an-y-time that I don't know what to do, I will

cast all my cares up-on you. ____

WORDS: Kelly Willard (Ps. 55:22; 1 Pet. 5:7)
MUSIC: Kelly Willard

© 1978 Maranatha Praise, Inc., admin. by The Copyright Co.

CARES CHORUS
Irregular

When We Are Called to Sing Your Praise 2216

1. When we are called to sing your praise with
2. When we are called to sing your praise and
3. When we are called to sing your praise and

hearts so filled with pain that we would rath - er
can - not find our voice, be - cause our los - ses
life a - head looks grim, still give us faith and

sit and weep or stand up to com - plain, re -
leave us now no rea - son to re - joice, re -
hope e - nough to break forth in a hymn, a

mind us, God, you un - der - stand the
mind us, God, that you ac - cept our
thank - ful hymn, great God of Love, that

bur - dens that we bear; you, too, have walked the
sad la - ments in prayer; you, too, have walked the
you are ev - ery - where; you walk the shad - owed

shad - owed way and known our deep de - spair.
shad - owed way and known our deep de - spair.
way with us and keep us in your care.

WORDS: Mary Nelson Keithahn
MUSIC: Trad. English melody

KINGSFOLD
CMD

Words © 2000 Abingdon Press, admin. by The Copyright Co.

2217

By the Babylonian Rivers

1. By the Bab - y - lo - nian riv - ers we sat
2. There our cap - tors in de - ri - sion did re -
3. How shall we sing the Lord's song in a

down in grief and wept; hung our harps up - on the
quire of us a song; so we sat with star - ing
strange and bit - ter land; can our voic - es veil the

wil - low, mourned for Zi - on when we slept.
vi - sion, and the days were hard and long.
sor - row? Lord God, help your ho - ly band.

WORDS: Ewald Bash (Ps. 137:1-4)
MUSIC: Trad. Latvian melody

KAS DZIEDAJA
87.87

Words © 1964 The American Lutheran Church, reprinted with permission of Augsburg Fortress

2218

You Are Mine

1. __ I will come to you in the si - lence, __
2. __ I am hope for all who are hope-less, __
3. __ I am strength for all the de - spair-ing, __
4. I am the Word that leads all to free - dom, I

I will lift you from __ all your fear. __
I am eyes for all who long to see. In the
heal - ing for the ones who dwell in shame. _____
am the peace the world can - not give. _____

WORDS: David Haas (Ps. 46:10; Isa. 43:1; John 14:27)
MUSIC: David Haas

YOU ARE MINE
Irregular with Refrain

© 1991 GIA Publications, Inc.

You will hear my voice, I claim you as my choice, be
shad-ows of the night, I will be your light,
All the blind will see, the lame will all run free, and
I will call your name, em - brac-ing all your pain, stand

still and know I am here. _____
come and rest in
all will know my
up, now walk, and

me. _____
name. _____
live! _____

Refrain

Do not be a-fraid, I am

with you. I have called you each by name.

Come and fol-low me, I will bring you home; I

love you and you are mine. _____

2219 Goodness Is Stronger than Evil

Good-ness is strong-er than e - vil; love is strong-er than
hate; light is strong-er than dark - ness; life is strong-er than
death. Vic-tory is ours, vic-tory is ours through him who
Oh, vic-tory is ours, vic-tory is ours

1.
loved us. Vic-tory is us.
through him who loved us. Oh, us.

WORDS: From *An African Prayer Book*, selected by Desmond Tutu
MUSIC: John Bell

GOODNESS IS STRONGER
Irregular

We Are God's People

1. We are God's peo - ple, the cho - sen of the
2. We are God's loved ones, the Bride of Christ, our
3. We are the bod - y of which the Lord is
4. We are a tem - ple, the Spir - it's dwell - ing

Lord, born of the Spir - it, es -
Lord, for we have known it, the
Head, called to o - bey Christ, now
place, formed in great weak - ness, a

tab - lished by the Word. Our cor - ner - stone is
love of God out - poured. Now let us learn how
ris - en from the dead. God wills us be a
cup to hold God's grace. We die a - lone, for

Christ a - lone, and strong in Christ we stand; O
to re - turn the gift of love once given; O
fam - i - ly di - verse, yet tru - ly one; O
on its own each em - ber los - es fire; yet

let us live trans - par - ent - ly and
let us share each joy and care and
let us give our gifts to God and
joined in one the flame burns on to

walk heart to heart and hand in hand.
live with a zeal that pleas - es heaven.
so shall God's work on earth be done.
give warmth and light and to in - spire.

WORDS: Bryan Jeffery Leech (John 3:5-8; 1 Cor. 3:16; Col. 1:18; 1 Pet. 2:9)
MUSIC: Johannes Brahms, adapt.

Words and adapt. © 1976 Fred Bock Music Co.

SYMPHONY
11 11 13.89

2221   In Unity We Lift Our Song

1. In u-ni-ty we lift our song of grate-ful a-dor-
2. For sto-ries told and told a-gain to ev-ery gen-er-
3. For sa-cred scrip-tures hand-ed down, a bless-ed trust and
4. For God our way, our bread, our rest, of all these gifts the

a - tion, for broth-ers brave and sis-ters strong. What
a - tion, to give us strength in times of pain, to
trea - sure, which give us hope when hope is gone and
Giv - er. Our strength, our guide, our nur-turing breast whose

cause for cel-e-bra - tion! For those whose faith-ful-ness
give us con-so-la - tion. Our spir-its to re-vive
make us weep with plea - sure. And when our eyes grow blind
hand will yet de-liv - er. Who keeps us till the day

has kept us through dis-tress, who've shared with us our plight,
to keep our dreams a - live, when we are far from home
and death is close be-hind, we shall re-cite them still
when night shall pass a-way, when hate and fear are gone

WORDS: Ken Medema
MUSIC: Martin Luther; harm. from *The New Hymnal for American Youth*

EIN' FESTE BURG
87.87.66.667

The Servant Song 2222

who've held us in the night, the bless-ed con-gre-ga - tion.
and e - vil sea-sons come; how firm is our foun-da - tion.
whose words our hearts can fill with hope be-yond all mea - sure.
and all our work is done, and we shall sing for-ev - er.

1., 6. Broth-er, sis - ter, let me serve you, let me be as
2. We are pil-grims on a jour-ney; we're to-geth - er
3. I will hold the Christ-light for you in the night-time
4. I will weep when you are weep-ing; when you laugh, I'll
5. When we sing to God in heav-en, we shall find such

Christ to you; pray that I may have the grace to
on this road. We are here to help each oth - er
of your fear; I will hold my hand out to you,
laugh with you. I will share your joy and sor - row
har - mo - ny, born of all we've known to - geth - er

let you be my ser - vant, too.
walk the mile and bear the load.
speak the peace you long to hear.
till we've seen this jour - ney through.
of Christ's love and ag - o - ny.

WORDS: Richard Gillard (Matt. 20:26)
MUSIC: Richard Gillard

THE SERVANT SONG
87.87

© 1977 Scripture in Song (a div. of Integrity Music, Inc.)

2223 They'll Know We Are Christians by Our Love

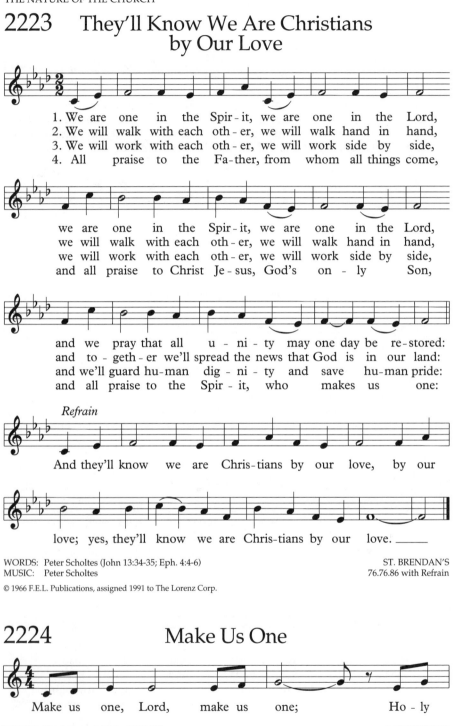

1. We are one in the Spir-it, we are one in the Lord,
2. We will walk with each oth-er, we will walk hand in hand,
3. We will work with each oth-er, we will work side by side,
4. All praise to the Fa-ther, from whom all things come,

we are one in the Spir-it, we are one in the Lord,
we will walk with each oth-er, we will walk hand in hand,
we will work with each oth-er, we will work side by side,
and all praise to Christ Je-sus, God's on-ly Son,

and we pray that all u-ni-ty may one day be re-stored:
and to-geth-er we'll spread the news that God is in our land:
and we'll guard hu-man dig-ni-ty and save hu-man pride:
and all praise to the Spir-it, who makes us one:

Refrain

And they'll know we are Chris-tians by our love, by our

love; yes, they'll know we are Chris-tians by our love. _____

WORDS: Peter Scholtes (John 13:34-35; Eph. 4:4-6)
MUSIC: Peter Scholtes

ST. BRENDAN'S
76.76.86 with Refrain

© 1966 F.E.L. Publications, assigned 1991 to The Lorenz Corp.

2224 Make Us One

Make us one, Lord, make us one; Ho-ly

WORDS: Carol Cymbala (John 17:22-23)
MUSIC: Carol Cymbala

MAKE US ONE
Irregular

© 1991 Word Music, Inc. and Carol Joy Music c/o Integrated Copyright Group

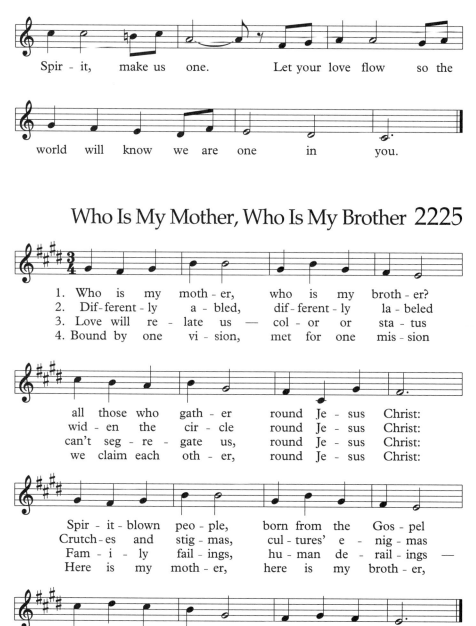

Spir - it, make us one. Let your love flow so the

world will know we are one in you.

Who Is My Mother, Who Is My Brother 2225

1. Who is my moth - er, who is my broth - er?
2. Dif - fer - ent - ly a - bled, dif - fer - ent - ly la - beled
3. Love will re - late us — col - or or sta - tus
4. Bound by one vi - sion, met for one mis - sion

all those who gath - er round Je - sus Christ:
wid - en the cir - cle round Je - sus Christ:
can't seg - re - gate us, round Je - sus Christ:
we claim each oth - er, round Je - sus Christ:

Spir - it - blown peo - ple, born from the Gos - pel
Crutch - es and stig - mas, cul - tures' e - nig - mas
Fam - i - ly fail - ings, hu - man de - rail - ings —
Here is my moth - er, here is my broth - er,

sit at the ta - ble, round Je - sus Christ.
all come to - geth - er round Je - sus Christ.
all are ac - cept - ed, round Je - sus Christ.
kin - dred in Spir - it, through Je - sus Christ.

WORDS: Shirley Erena Murray (Matt. 12:46-50; Mark 3:31-35; Luke 8:19-21)
MUSIC: Jack Schrader

KINDRED
54.54 D

2226 Bind Us Together

Bind us to-geth-er, Lord, bind us to-geth-er with cords that
can-not be bro - ken. Bind us to - geth - er, Lord,

Fine

bind us to-geth-er, Lord, bind us to-geth-er in love. ____

There is on-ly one God, ____ there is on-ly one King; ____

D.C. al Fine

There is on-ly one bod-y, ____ that is why we sing. ____

WORDS: Bob Gillman (Col. 3:14)
MUSIC: Bob Gillman

BIND US TOGETHER
Irregular

© 1977 Kingsway's Thank You Music

2227 We Are the Body of Christ

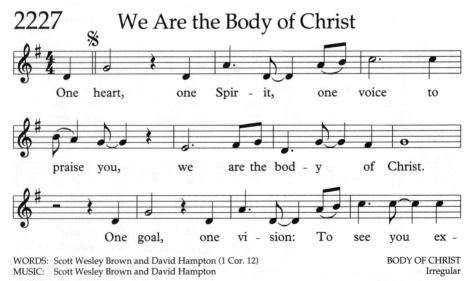

One heart, one Spir - it, one voice to
praise you, we are the bod - y of Christ.
One goal, one vi - sion: To see you ex -

WORDS: Scott Wesley Brown and David Hampton (1 Cor. 12)
MUSIC: Scott Wesley Brown and David Hampton

BODY OF CHRIST
Irregular

© 1996 New Spring Publishing, Inc. (a div. of Brentwood-Benson Music Publishing, Inc.); and SongWard Music,
admin. by The Copyright Co.; and ThreeFold Amen Music, admin. by ROM Administration

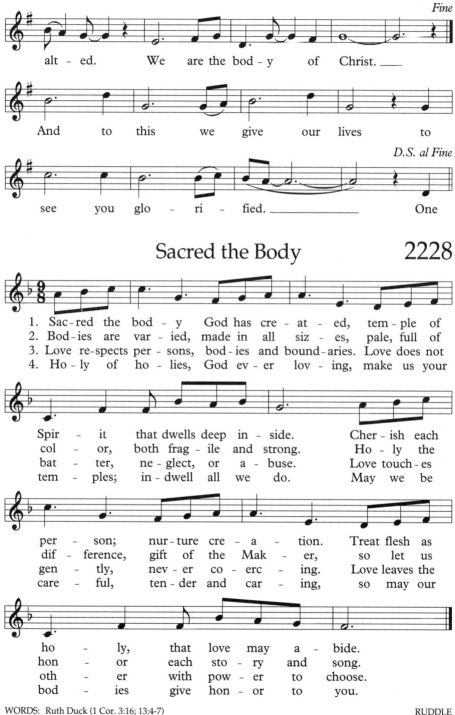

Fine

alt - ed. We are the bod - y of Christ. ____

And to this we give our lives to

D.S. al Fine

see you glo - ri - fied. ____ One

Sacred the Body 2228

1. Sac-red the bod - y God has cre - at - ed, tem - ple of
2. Bod-ies are var - ied, made in all siz - es, pale, full of
3. Love re-spects per - sons, bod-ies and bound-aries. Love does not
4. Ho - ly of ho - lies, God ev - er lov - ing, make us your

Spir - it that dwells deep in - side. Cher - ish each
col - or, both frag - ile and strong. Ho - ly the
bat - ter, ne - glect, or a - buse. Love touch-es
tem - ples; in - dwell all we do. May we be

per - son; nur-ture cre - a - tion. Treat flesh as
dif - ference, gift of the Mak - er, so let us
gen - tly, nev - er co - erc - ing. Love leaves the
care - ful, ten - der and car - ing, so may our

ho - ly, that love may a - bide.
hon - or each sto - ry and song.
oth - er with pow - er to choose.
bod - ies give hon - or to you.

WORDS: Ruth Duck (1 Cor. 3:16; 13:4-7)
MUSIC: W. Daniel Landes

RUDDLE
10 10.10 10

2229 We Are One in Christ Jesus
(Somos Uno en Cristo)

We are one in Christ Je-sus, all one bod-y, all one
So-mos u-no en Cris-to, so-mos u-no, so-mos

spir-it, all to-geth-er. We are geth-er. We share one
u-no, u-no só-lo. So-mos só-lo. Un so-lo

God, one might-y Lord, one a-bid-ing
Dios, un so-lo Se-ñor, u-na so-la

faith, one bind-ing love, one sin-gle bap-ti-sm, one Ho-ly
fe, un so-lo a-mor, un so-lo bau-tis-mo, un so-lo Es-

Com-fort-er, the Ho-ly Spir-it, u-nit-ing all.
pí-ri-tu y e-se es el Con-so-la-dor.

WORDS: Anon.; English trans. by Alice Parker (Eph. 4:4-6)   SOMOS UNO
MUSIC: Anon.   Irregular

Trans. © 1996 Abingdon Press, admin. by The Copyright Co.

2230 Lord, We Come to Ask Your Blessing

1. Lord, we come to ask your bless - ing
2. God of love, un - less you bless us
3. May our lov - ing be a shar - ing
4. Lord, we come to ask your bless - ing

WORDS: Fred Pratt Green   SUGAR GROVE
MUSIC: W. Daniel Landes   87.87

Words © 1989 Hope Publishing Co.; music © 1997 Abingdon Press, admin. by The Copyright Co.

on the love that makes us one;
how can we each oth - er bless?
of the gifts we each pos - sess;
in the pres - ence of our friends:

here, as Chris-tians, to ac-
On - ly as you live with-
may no fail - ure of for-
Grant us joy that bless-es

knowl - edge you are Lord, and you a - lone.
in us is there depth of hap - pi - ness.
bear - ance turn our love to bit - ter - ness.
oth - ers, grant us love that nev - er ends.

O Look and Wonder 2231
(¡Miren Qué Bueno!)

Refrain
Last time: Fine

O look and won - der, how good it is!
¡Mi - ren qué bue - no, qué bue - no es!

1., 2., 3. Look at how good it is for us to be here all to - geth - er,
1. Mi-ren qué bue-no es cuan-do los her - ma-nos es-tán jun - tos,
2. Mi-ren qué bue-no es cuan-do las her - ma-nas es-tán jun - tas,
3. Mi-ren qué bue-no es cuan-do nos reu - ni-mos to-dos jun - tos,

D.C.

it is like pre-cious oil that runs from Aa-ron's head and beard.
it is like He-bron's dew that falls up - on the hills of Zion.
it is the prom-ise of the Lord e - ter-nal - ly to bless.
es co-mo a-cei - te bue - no de - rra - ma - do so-bre Aa - rón.
se pa - re-ce al ro - cí - o so - bre los mon - tes de Sion.
por-que el Se - ñor ahí man-da vi - da e - ter-na y ben - di - ción.

WORDS: Pablo Sosa; English trans. by George Lockwood (Ps. 133)
MUSIC: Pablo Sosa

MIREN QUÉ BUENO
Irregular with Refrain

2232 Come Now, O Prince of Peace
(O-So-So)

1. Come now, O Prince of Peace, make us one bod-y,
2. Come now, O God of love, make us one bod-y,

1. *O - so - so   o - so - so,   pyong-hwa eui   im - gum*
2. *O - so - so   o - so - so,   sa - rang eui   im - gum*

come, O Lord Je - sus, re-con-cile your peo - ple.
come, O Lord Je - sus, re-con-cile your peo - ple.

u - ri - ga   han - mom   i - ru - ge   ha - so - so.
u - ri - ga   han - mom   i - ru - ge   ha - so - so.

3. Come now and set us free,
   O God our Savior,
   come, O Lord Jesus,
   reconcile all nations.

3. *O-so-so o-so-so,*
   cha-yu eui im-gum,
   u-ri-ga han-mom
   i-ru-ge ha-so-so.

4. Come, Hope of unity,
   make us one body,
   come, O Lord Jesus,
   reconcile all nations.

4. *O-so-so o-so-so*
   tong-il eui im-gum,
   u-ri-ga han-mom
   i-ru-ge ha-so-so.

WORDS: Geonyong Lee; English paraphrase by Marion Pope (Isa. 9:6; John 17:22-23)
MUSIC: Geonyong Lee
© 1988 Geonyong Lee

GEONYONG
65.56

2233 Where Children Belong

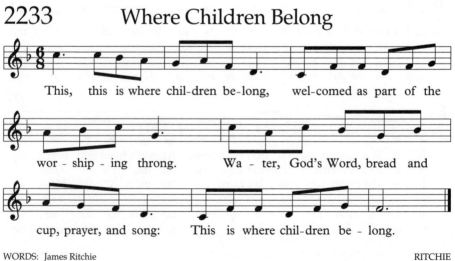

This, this is where chil-dren be-long, wel-comed as part of the

wor - ship - ing throng. Wa - ter, God's Word, bread and

cup, prayer, and song: This is where chil-dren be - long.

WORDS: James Ritchie
MUSIC: James Ritchie
© 1999 Abingdon Press, admin. by The Copyright Co.

RITCHIE
Irregular

Lead On, O Cloud of Presence

2234

1. Lead on, O cloud of Pres - ence, the ex - o - dus is come,
2. Lead on, O fier - y Pil - lar, we fol - low yet with fears,
3. Lead on, O God of free - dom, and guide us on our way,

in wil - der - ness and des - ert our tribe shall make its home.
but we shall come re - joic - ing though joy be born of tears.
and help us trust the prom - ise through strug - gle and de - lay.

Our slav - ery left be - hind us, new hopes with - in us grow.
We are not lost, though wan - dering, for by your light we come,
We pray our sons and daugh - ters may jour - ney to that land

We seek the land of prom - ise where milk and hon - ey flow.
and we are still God's peo - ple. The jour - ney is our home.
where jus - tice dwells with mer - cy, and love is law's de - mand.

WORDS: Ruth Duck (Exod. 13:21-22)
MUSIC: Henry T. Smart

LANCASHIRE
76.76 D

Words © 1992 GIA Publications, Inc.

2235-a

We Are Singing
(Siyahamba/Caminando)

Refrain (may be sung in unison throughout)

(English) We are sing - ing* for the
(Zulu**) See yah hahm buh koo kah
(Spanish) Ca - mi - nan - do en la

Lord is our light, we are sing-ing for the Lord is our light. _
nigh nee kwen kohs. See yah hahm buh koo kah nigh nee kwen kohs. _
luz de Dios, ca - mi - nan - do en la luz de Dios. _

1

2

Lord is our light. _
nigh nee kwen kohs. _
luz de Dios. _

We are sing - ing for the Lord is, for the
See yah hahm buh koo kah nigh nee, koo kah
Ca - mi - nan - do en la luz, en la

Lord is our light. _
nigh nee kwen kohs. _
luz de Dios. _

*marching, walking, ringing, dancing, praying
**Phonetic syllables; see 2235-b for original language.

WORDS: South Africa (20th cent.); adapt. by Hal H. Hopson
MUSIC: South Africa (20th cent.); acc. by Hal H. Hopson

SIYAHAMBA
Irregular

2235-b

We Are Marching
(Siyahamba/Caminando)

(English) We are march - ing* in the
(Zulu) Si - ya - hamb' e - ku - kha -
(Spanish) Ca - mi - nan - do en la

light of God, we are march-ing in the light of God.
nyen' kwen - khos', si - ya - hamb' e - ku - kha-nyen' kwen - khos.
luz de Dios, ca - mi - nan - do en la luz de Dios.

of God
kwen - khos'
de Dios

We are march-ing in the light of, the
Si - ya - hamb' e - ku - kha-nyen' kwen kha -
Ca - mi - nan - do en la luz de, la

of God
kwen - khos'
de Dios

*singing, walking, ringing, dancing, praying, etc.

WORDS: South Africa (20th cent.)
MUSIC: South Africa (20th cent.)

SIYAHAMBA
Irregular

2236

Gather Us In

1. Here in this place new light is stream-ing,
2. We are the young — our lives are a mys-t'ry,
3. Here we will take the wine and the wa-ter,
4. Not in the dark of build-ings con-fin-ing,

now is the dark-ness van-ished a-way,
we are the old — who yearn for your face,
here we will take the bread of new birth,
not in some heav-en, light-years a-way, but

see in this space our fears and our dream-ings,
we have been sung through-out all of his-t'ry,
here you shall call your sons and your daugh-ters,
here in this place the new light is shin-ing,

brought here to you in the light of this day. ____
called to be light to the whole hu-man race. ____
call us a-new to be salt for the earth. ____
now is the King-dom, now is the day. ____

Gath-er us in — the lost and for-sak-en, gath-er us in — the
Gath-er us in — the rich and the haugh-ty, gath-er us in — the
Give us to drink the wine of com-pas-sion, give us to eat the
Gath-er us in and hold us for-ev-er, gath-er us in and

blind and the lame; call to us now, and we shall a-wak-en,
proud and the strong; give us a heart so meek and so low-ly,
bread that is you; nour-ish us well, and teach us to fash-ion
make us your own; gath-er us in — all peo-ples to-geth-er,

WORDS: Marty Haugen (Matt. 5:13)
MUSIC: Marty Haugen

GATHER US IN
Irregular

we shall a - rise at the sound of our name. _____
give us the cour-age to en - ter the song. _____
lives that are ho - ly and hearts that are true. _____
fire of love in our flesh and our bone. _____

As a Fire Is Meant for Burning   2237

1. As a fire is meant for burn - ing with a bright and warm-ing
2. We are learn - ers; we are teach - ers; we are pil - grims on the
3. As a green bud in the spring-time is a sign of life re -

flame, so the church is meant for mis - sion, giv - ing
way. We are seek - ers; we are giv - ers; we are
newed, so may we be signs of one - ness 'mid earth's

glo - ry to God's name. Not to preach our creeds or
ves - sels made of clay. By our gen - tle, lov - ing
peo - ples, man - y hued. As a rain - bow lights the

cus - toms, but to build a bridge of care, we join
ac - tions we would show that Christ is light. In a
heav - ens when a storm is past and gone, may our

hands a - cross the na - tions, find-ing neigh-bors ev - ery-where.
hum - ble, lis-tening Spir - it we would live to God's de - light.
lives re - flect the ra - diance of God's new and glo-rious dawn.

WORDS: Ruth Duck
MUSIC: From *The Sacred Harp*, 1844
Words © 1992 GIA Publications, Inc.

BEACH SPRING
87.87 D

2238 In the Midst of New Dimensions

1. In the midst of new di - men-sions, in the face of
2. Through the flood of starv - ing peo - ple, war - ring fac - tions
3. As we stand a world di - vid - ed by our own self -
4. We are man and we are wom - an, all per - sua - sions,
5. Should the threats of dire pre - dic - tions cause us to with -

chang - ing ways, who will lead the pil - grim peo - ples
and de - spair, who will lift the ol - ive branch - es?
seek - ing schemes, grant that we, your glob - al vil - lage,
old and young, each a gift in your cre - a - tion,
draw in pain, may your blaz - ing phoe - nix spir - it

Refrain

wan-dering in their sep-arate ways?
Who will light the flame of care?
might en - vi - sion wid - er dreams. God of rain-bow, fier - y pil - lar,
each a love song to be sung.
res - ur - rect the church a - gain.

lead-ing where the ea-gles soar, we your peo-ple, ours the jour-ney

WORDS: Julian B. Rush (Gen. 9:12-16; Exod. 13:21-22; Num. 14:14)　　　NEW DIMENSIONS
MUSIC: Julian B. Rush　　　87.87 with Refrain

© 1994 Julian B. Rush

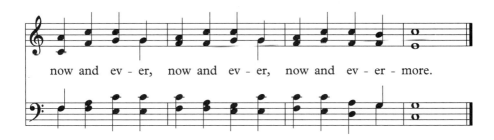

now and ev - er, now and ev - er, now and ev - er - more.

Go Ye, Go Ye into the World 2239

Descant

3. Go ye now and

Melody

1.-3. Go ye, go ye in - to the world, and

tell the sto - ry to all be - liev - ers. Go ye

make dis - ci - ples of all the na - tions.
take the gos - pel to all the peo - ple.
tell the sto - ry to all be - liev - ers.
Go ye, go ye

now, and I will be with you there!

in - to the world, and I will be with you there!

WORDS: Natalie Sleeth (Matt. 28:18-20)
MUSIC: Natalie Sleeth
© 1979 Choristers Guild

GO YE, GO YE
8 10.87

2240 One God and Father of Us All

1. All the gifts that God has giv- en by his
(2. There are) dif-ferenc-es a- mong us God can

grace to ev - ery - one were
use to make us strong. Our

meant to give us each a place to serve. __ And if
tap-es-try, his liv - ing work of art. ___ In the

we will come to-geth - er to see his will be done, we will
love that u - ni-fies us by the faith that leads us on, we can

Refrain

share in bless - ings more than we de - serve. There is
fol - low with one pur - pose and one heart.

one God and Fa-ther of us all, a - bove all and through all and

in all. In the bond of ho - ly u - ni-ty with our

spir-its joined as one, let us live lives wor - thy of the

WORDS: Pete Carlson and Kyle Matthews (Eph. 4:6-7)
MUSIC: Pete Carlson and Kyle Matthews

ONE GOD
Irregular with Refrain

© 1999 New Spring Publishing, Inc./Matters Most Music and BMG Songs, Inc./Above the Rim Music

The Spirit Sends Us Forth to Serve 2241

1. The Spir - it sends us forth to serve; we
2. We go to com - fort those who mourn and
3. We go to be the hands of Christ, to
4. Then let us go to serve in peace, the

go in Je - sus' name to bring glad tid - ings
set the bur - dened free; where hope is dim, to
scat - ter joy like seed and, all our days, to
gos - pel to pro - claim. God's Spir - it has em -

to the poor, God's fa - vor to pro - claim.
share a dream and help the blind to see.
cher - ish life, to do the lov - ing deed.
pow - ered us; we go in Je - sus' name.

WORDS: Delores Dufner, OSB
MUSIC: USA folk melody
LAND OF REST
CM

Words © 1993 Delores Dufner, admin. by OCP Publications

2242

Walk with Me

WORDS: John S. Rice (Exod. 3:1–4:20; Matt. 16:13-20; Mark 16:9)
MUSIC: John S. Rice

GLASER
CM with Refrain

© 1988 The Estate of John S. Rice

D.C.

"You're the one to set my peo-ple free."
ho - li - ness and he be-came the Rock.
dared to let God's love un - lock the door.
faith - ful-ness calls me to walk with you.

We All Are One in Mission 2243

1. We all are one in mis - sion; we all are one in call,
2. We all are called for ser - vice, to wit-ness in God's name.
3. Now let us be u - nit - ed, and let our song be heard.

our var-ied gifts u - nit - ed by Christ, the Lord of all.
Our min-is-tries are dif-ferent; our pur - pose is the same:
Now let us be a ves - sel for God's re - deem-ing Word.

A sin - gle great com - mis - sion com - pels us from a - bove
To touch the lives of oth - ers by God's sur-pris-ing grace,
We all are one in mis - sion; we all are one in call,

to plan and work to - geth-er that all may know Christ's love.
so ev - ery folk and na-tion may feel God's warm em - brace.
our var - ied gifts u - nit-ed by Christ, the Lord of all.

WORDS: Rusty Edwards (Matt. 28:19-20; 1 Cor. 12:4-6)
MUSIC: Finnish folk melody

KUORTANE
76.76 D

2244 People Need the Lord

1. Peo-ple need the Lord, peo-ple need the
2. Peo-ple need the Lord, peo-ple need the

Lord; at the end of bro - ken dreams,
Lord; when will we re - al - ize

1 he's the o - pen door.

2 peo-ple need the Lord.

WORDS: Greg Nelson and Phill McHugh (John 4:35; 10:7)
MUSIC: Greg Nelson and Phill McHugh

PEOPLE NEED THE LORD
Irregular

2245 Within the Day-to-Day
(A Hymn for Deacons)

1. With - in the day - to - day, a - mong the "A"-through-
(2. The) pal - ace has its place, mu - se - ums play their
(3. The) sur-geon sews the heart, the plumb-er tends the
(4. The) ex - ca - vat - ing God un - earths new hope each

"Z," there is a world of mir - a - cles which
part; but chil-dren's sim - ple, hand-made gifts are
leak; but who can match the lov - ing kiss up -
day, and trusts the mir - a - cle of life to

1 God calls us to see. 2. The
pre-cious, God - ly art. 3. The
on a tear-stained cheek? 4. The

2 us, the soul-filled clay.

WORDS: John Thornburg
MUSIC: Jane Marshall

TWENTY
SM

Deep in the Shadows of the Past 2246

1. Deep in the shad-ows of the past, far
2. While oth-ers bowed to change-less gods they
3. From Ex-o-dus to Pen-te-cost the
4. For all the writ-ings that sur-vived, for

out from set-tled lands, some no-mads trav-eled
met a mys-ter-y, in-vis-i-ble, with-
prom-ise changed and grew, while some, re-mem-ber-
lead-ers, long a-go, who sift-ed, cop-ied,

with their God a - cross the des-ert
out a name: "I AM WHAT I WILL
ing the past, re-cord-ed what they
and pre-served the Bi-ble that we

sands. The dawn-ing hope of hu-man-kind by
BE"; and by their tents, a-round their fires, in
knew, or with their let-ters and la-ments, their
know, give thanks, and find its sto-ry yet our

them was sensed and shown; a prom-ise call-ing
sto-ry, song and law, they praised, re-mem-bered,
proph-e-cy and praise re-cov-ered, kin-dled
prom-ise, strength and call, the mod-el of e -

them a-head, a fu-ture yet un-known.
hand-ed on a past that prom-ised more.
and ex-pressed new hope for chang-ing days.
merg-ing faith, a-live with hope for all.

WORDS: Brian Wren
MUSIC: English melody
Words © 1975, 1995 Hope Publishing Co.

KINGSFOLD
CMD

2247 Wonder of Wonders

1. Won - der of won - ders, here re - vealed;
2. Here in this sac - ra - ment we see
3. This child of God, though young or old,
4. Now we our vow of faith re - new,

God's cov - e - nant with us is sealed.
God's grace un - bound, for all, for me!
we wel - come now in - to Christ's fold,
stretch wide our sights to glob - al view,

And long be - fore we know or pray,
May we re - spond with joy - ful praise
to know with us God's lov - ing care;
and claim with Chris - tians far and near

God's love en - folds us ev - ery day.
in lov - ing ser - vice all our days.
here all our joys and sor - rows share.
a larg - er fam - i - ly held dear.

WORDS: Jane Parker Huber
MUSIC: William Boyd

PENTECOST
LM

Baptized in Water

2248

1. Bap-tized in wa - ter, sealed by the Spir - it, cleansed by the
2. Bap-tized in wa - ter, sealed by the Spir - it, dead in the
3. Bap-tized in wa - ter, sealed by the Spir - it, marked with the

blood of Christ, our King; heirs of sal - va - tion, trust-ing his
tomb with Christ, our King; one with his ris - ing, freed and for -
sign of Christ, our King; born of one Fa - ther, we are his

prom - ise, faith-ful - ly now God's prais-es we sing.
giv - en, thank-ful - ly now God's prais-es we sing.
chil - dren, joy-ful - ly now God's prais-es we sing.

WORDS: Michael Saward (Rom. 6:3-5)
MUSIC: Trad. Gaelic melody

BUNESSAN
55.54 D

Words © 1982 Jubilate Hymns, admin. by Hope Publishing Co.

God Claims You

2249

Refrain*

**"Dan - iel, Dan - iel," God claims you, God helps you, pro -
Child of prom - ise,
Fine

tects you, and loves you, too.
1. We this day do
***2. We your fam - ily
3. We are here to
4. And if you should

D.C.

all a - gree a child of God you'll al - ways be.
love you so, we vow to help your faith to grow.
say this day that we will help you on your way.
tire or cry then we will sing this lul - la - by.

*Sing Refrain twice at beginning and end, and once between stanzas.
**May insert child's name.
***May insert parents' names "Jeff and Kathy love you so, we vow ..."

WORDS: Stanley M. Farr
MUSIC: Stanley M. Farr

FARR
Irregular with Refrain

© 1981 Stanley M. Farr

2250 I've Just Come from the Fountain

WORDS: African American spiritual
MUSIC: African American spiritual; arr. by James Capers

HIS NAME SO SWEET
88.74 with Refrain

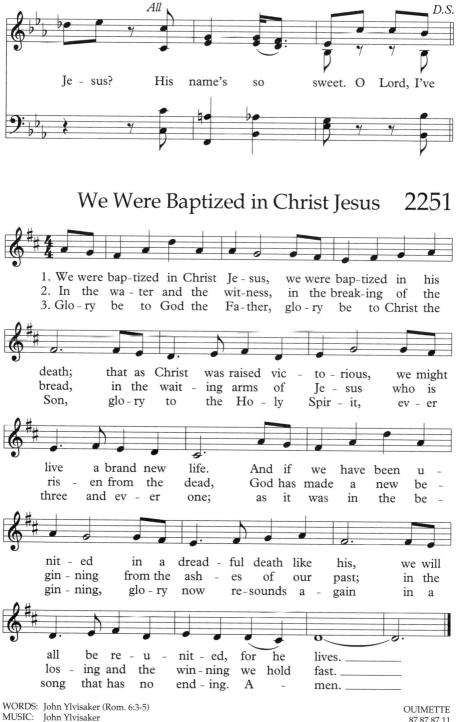

We Were Baptized in Christ Jesus   2251

1. We were bap-tized in Christ Je - sus, we were bap-tized in his
2. In the wa - ter and the wit-ness, in the break-ing of the
3. Glo - ry be to God the Fa-ther, glo - ry be to Christ the

death; that as Christ was raised vic - to - rious, we might
bread, in the wait - ing arms of Je - sus who is
Son, glo - ry to the Ho - ly Spir - it, ev - er

live a brand new life. And if we have been u -
ris - en from the dead, God has made a new be -
three and ev - er one; as it was in the be -

nit - ed in a dread - ful death like his, we will
gin - ning from the ash - es of our past; in the
gin - ning, glo - ry now re-sounds a - gain in a

all be re - u - nit - ed, for he lives. _____
los - ing and the win - ning we hold fast. _____
song that has no end - ing. A - men. _____

WORDS: John Ylvisaker (Rom. 6:3-5)
MUSIC: John Ylvisaker

OUIMETTE
87.87.87.11

2252   Come, Be Baptized

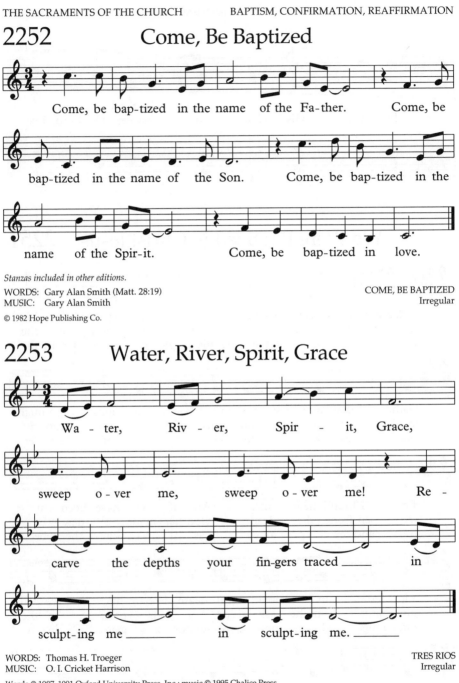

Come, be bap-tized in the name of the Fa-ther. Come, be

bap-tized in the name of the Son. Come, be bap-tized in the

name of the Spir-it. Come, be bap-tized in love.

Stanzas included in other editions.

WORDS: Gary Alan Smith (Matt. 28:19)
MUSIC: Gary Alan Smith

COME, BE BAPTIZED
Irregular

© 1982 Hope Publishing Co.

2253   Water, River, Spirit, Grace

Wa - ter,   Riv - er,   Spir - it,   Grace,

sweep   o - ver   me,   sweep   o - ver   me!   Re -

carve   the   depths   your   fin-gers traced _____   in

sculpt-ing me _____   in   sculpt-ing   me. _____

WORDS: Thomas H. Troeger
MUSIC: O. I. Cricket Harrison

TRES RIOS
Irregular

Words © 1987, 1991 Oxford University Press, Inc.; music © 1995 Chalice Press

BAPTISM, CONFIRMATION, REAFFIRMATION, *see further:*

In Remembrance of Me

2254

1. In re - mem-brance of me, eat this bread. ___ In re -
(2. In re -) mem-brance of me, heal the sick. ___ In re -
(3. In re -) mem-brance of me, search for truth. ___ In re -

mem-brance of me, drink this wine. ___ In re-mem-brance of
mem-brance of me, feed the poor. ___ In re-mem-brance of
mem-brance of me, al - ways love. ___ In re-mem-brance of

Third time to Coda

me, pray for the time when God's own will is
me, o - pen the door and let your neigh - bors
me, don't look a - bove, but in your

done. ___ 2. In re - in, let them in. ___ Take,

eat, and be com - fort - ed; drink and re - mem - ber,

too, ___ that this is my bod - y and pre - cious

D.S. al Coda

blood shed for you, ___ shed for you. ___ 3. In re -

CODA

heart, ___ look for God. ___

Do this in re - mem-brance of me. ___

WORDS: Ragan Courtney (Matt. 6:10; 1 Cor. 11:23-25)
MUSIC: Buryl Red

RED
Irregular

2255 In the Singing

1. In the sing-ing, in the si-lence, in the hands ex-pec-tant,
2. In the ques-tion, in the an-swer, in the mo-ment of ac -

o - pen, in the bless - ing, in the break-ing,
cep - tance, in the heart's cry, in the heal - ing,

in the Pres - ence at this ta - ble —
in the cir - cle of your peo - ple —

Refrain

Je - sus Christ, Je - sus Christ, be the wine of grace:

Je - sus Christ, Je - sus Christ, be the bread of peace.

WORDS: Shirley Erena Murray
MUSIC: Carlton R. Young

BREAD OF PEACE
LM with Refrain

© 1996 Hope Publishing Co.

2256 Holy, Holy, Holy Lord
(Sanctus)

Part 1

1. Ho - ly, ho - ly, ho - ly Lord of
(2. Bless-ed,) bless-ed is he who comes in the

Part 2

1. Ho - ly, _____ ho - ly, ho - ly Lord of
(2. Bless-ed,) _____ bless-ed is he who comes in the

WORDS: Trad. (Isa. 6:3; Matt. 21:9)
MUSIC: Iona Community (Scotland)

SANCTUS (IONA)
Irregular

© WGRG The Iona Community (Scotland), admin. by GIA Publications, Inc.

2257-a   Communion Setting
(Preface)

The Lord be with you. _____ And al - so with you. _____ Lift up your hearts. _____ We lift them up to the Lord. _____ Let us give thanks to the Lord our God. It is right to give our thanks and praise. _____

WORDS: From *The United Methodist Hymnal*
MUSIC: Mark A. Miller

Music © 2000 Abingdon Press, admin. by The Copyright Co.

2257-b   (Sanctus)

Ho - ly, ho - ly, ho - ly Lord; God of power and might. _____ Heav - en and earth are

WORDS: From *The United Methodist Hymnal* (Isa. 6:3; Matt. 21:9)
MUSIC: Mark A. Miller

Music © 1999 Abingdon Press, admin. by The Copyright Co.

2257-c   (Memorial Acclamation)

Christ has died, Christ is ris - en,
Christ will come a - gain. _____ Ho -
san - na in the high-est! Ho - san - na in the high-est! Ho -
san - na in the high - est! _____

WORDS: From *The United Methodist Hymnal*
MUSIC: Mark A. Miller

Music © 1999 Abingdon Press, admin. by The Copyright Co.

2257-d   (Great Amen)

A - men. A - men. A -
men. _____ Ho - san - na in the high-est! Ho - san - na in the
high - est! Ho - san - na in the high - est! _____

WORDS: From *The United Methodist Hymnal*
MUSIC: Mark A. Miller

Music © 1999 Abingdon Press, admin. by The Copyright Co.

Sing Alleluia to the Lord

2258

2. Lift up your hearts unto the Lord …
3. In Christ the world has been redeemed …
4. His resurrection sets us free …
5. Therefore we celebrate the feast …
6. Sing alleluia to the Lord …

WORDS: Sts. 1, 6 by Linda Stassen; sts. 2-5 from early Christian liturgy (1 Cor. 5:8)
MUSIC: Linda Stassen

SING ALLELUIA
Irregular

2259   Victim Divine

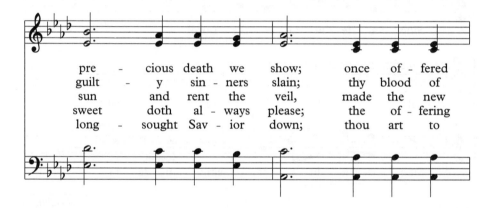

1. Vic - tim Di - vine, thy grace we claim while thus thy
2. Thou stand - est in the ho - liest place, as now for
3. The smoke of thy a - tone - ment here dark - ened the
4. He still re - spects thy sac - ri - fice, its sa - vor
5. We need not go up to heav - en, to bring the

pre - cious death we show; once of - fered
guilt - y sin - ners slain; thy blood of
sun and rent the veil, made the new
sweet doth al - ways please; the of - fering
long - sought Sav - ior down; thou art to

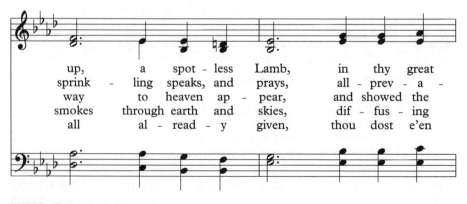

up, a spot - less Lamb, in thy great
sprink - ling speaks, and prays, all - prev - a -
way to heaven ap - pear, and showed the
smokes through earth and skies, dif - fus - ing
all al - read - y given, thou dost e'en

WORDS: Charles Wesley (Heb. 10:12-22)   SELENA
MUSIC: Isaac B. Woodbury   88.88.88

tem - ple here be - low, thou didst for all our kind a -
lent for help-less ones; thy blood is still our ran - som
great In - vis - i - ble; well pleased in thee our God looked
life, and joy, and peace; to these thy low - er courts it
now thy ban-quet crown: To ev - ery faith - ful soul ap -

tone, and stand - est now be - fore the throne.
found, and spreads sal - va - tion all a - round.
down, and called his reb - els to a crown.
comes, and fills them with di - vine per - fumes.
pear, and show thy real pres - ence here!

Let Us Be Bread 2260

Let us be bread, blessed by the Lord, bro - ken and

shared, life for the world. Let us be wine,

love free - ly poured. Let us be one in the Lord. _____

Stanzas included in other editions.

WORDS: Thomas Porter
MUSIC: Thomas Porter

© 1990 GIA Publications, Inc.

LET US BE BREAD
Irregular

2261 Life-giving Bread

Life - giv - ing bread, _____ as our hearts are trans -
formed a - new, _____ and life - giv - ing wine, ___
_ may we share in a life with you. _____

Stanzas included in other editions.
WORDS: Ricky Manalo (John 6:35, 48)
MUSIC: Ricky Manalo
© 1994 GIA Publications, Inc.

MANALO
Irregular

2262 Let Us Offer to the Father
(Te Ofrecemos Padre Nuestro)

Refrain

Let us of - fer to the Fa - ther, with the bread and with the
Te o-fre - ce - mos, Pa - dre nues-tro, con el vi - no y con el

wine, all our joys and all our sor - rows; all our
pan, nues-tras pe - nas y a - le - grí - as, el tra -

[1-4 / to stanzas] [5] *Fine*

cares, Lord, all are thine. cares, Lord, all are thine.
ba - jo y nues - tro a - fán. ba - jo y nues - tro a - fán.

WORDS: From the *Misa Popular Nicaragüense*; trans. by Alice Parker
MUSIC: From the *Misa Popular Nicaragüense*; arr. by Raquel Mora Martínez
Trans. and arr. © 1994 Abingdon Press, admin. by The Copyright Co.

OFERTORIO
87.87 with Refrain

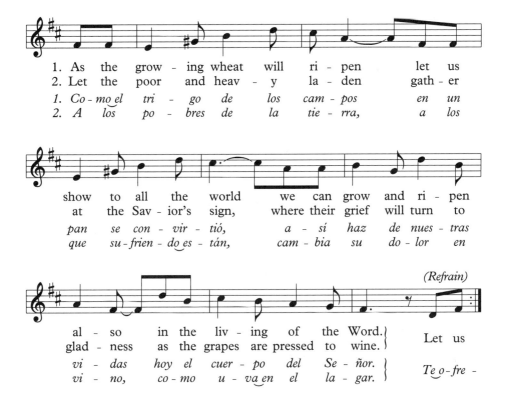

1. As the grow - ing wheat will ri - pen let us
2. Let the poor and heav - y la - den gath - er
1. Co - mo el tri - go de los cam - pos en un
2. A los po - bres de la tie - rra, a los

show to all the world we can grow and ri - pen
at the Sav - ior's sign, where their grief will turn to
pan se con - vir - tió, a - sí haz de nues - tras
que su - frien - do es - tán, cam - bia su do - lor en

(Refrain)

al - so in the liv - ing of the Word.⎱
glad - ness as the grapes are pressed to wine.⎰ Let us
vi - das hoy el cuer - po del Se - ñor. ⎱
vi - no, co - mo u - va en el la - gar. ⎰ Te o - fre -

3. From the country, from the city,
   from the riches of the land,
   we bring back to our Creator
   many gifts of heart and hand.

4. All your people here together
   bring you offerings of love,
   joining with your whole creation,
   seeking liberty and peace.

5. Glory be to God, the Father
   and to Christ, the living Son,
   who together with the Spirit
   make the holy Three-in-One.

3. *Estos dones son el signo*
   del esfuerzo de unidad
   que la humanidad realiza
   en el campo y la ciudad.

4. *Es tu pueblo quien te ofrece,*
   con los dones del altar,
   la naturaleza entera,
   anhelando libertad.

5. *Gloria sea dada al Padre*
   y a su Hijo Redentor
   y al Espíritu Divino
   que nos llena de su amor.

2263 Broken for Me

Last time to Coda

Refrain

Bro-ken for me, _____ bro-ken for you,

the bod-y of Je - sus, _____ bro-ken for you.

1. He of-fered his bod - y; _____ he poured out his soul;
2. _ Come to my ta - ble _____ _ and with me dine;
3. _ This is my bod - y _____ _ giv - en for you;
4. _ This is my blood _____ _ I shed for you,

D.C.

Je - sus was bro - ken _____ that we might be whole.
eat of my bread _____ and drink of my wine.
eat it, re-mem - bering _ _ I died for you.
for your for-give - ness, _____ _ mak-ing you new.

CODA

the bod-y of Je - sus, _____ bro-ken for you.

WORDS: Janet Lunt (1 Cor. 11:23-25)
MUSIC: Janet Lunt

© 1978 Sovereign Music UK

BROKEN FOR ME
Irregular with Refrain

2264 Come to the Table

Come to the ta-ble of mer - cy, pre-pared with the wine and the

bread. All who are hun-gry and thirst - y,

WORDS: Claire Cloninger
MUSIC: Martin J. Nystrom

© 1991 Word Music, Inc. and Integrity's Hosanna! Music

TABLE OF MERCY
Irregular

come and your souls will be fed. Come at the Lord's in - vi -

ta - tion; re - ceive from his nail - scarred hand.

Eat of the bread of sal - va - tion; drink of the blood of the Lamb.

Time Now to Gather 2265

1. Time now to gath - er, time now to feel
2. Time to re - mem - ber Christ who was sent.
3. All who are hun - gry, come, and be fed.

Christ's ho - ly pres - ence grac - ing this meal.
Time to say, "Thank you" for all he meant.
Serve one an - oth - er this cup and bread.

Grain from the har - vest, fruit of the vine;
Come to this ta - ble. Come, with - out fear.
All who are trou - bled, hurt - ing, or sad,

sim - ple the sup - per, sa - cred the sign.
God will for - give you, wel - come you here.
come, and find heal - ing. Come, and be glad!

WORDS: Mary Nelson Keithahn (Luke 22:19-20)
MUSIC: John D. Horman

WELCOME SONG
54.54 D

© 1998 Abingdon Press, admin. by The Copyright Co.

2266 Here Is Bread, Here Is Wine

1. Here is bread, here is wine: ⎫
2. Here is grace, here is peace: ⎬ Christ is with us:
3. Here we are, joined in one: ⎭

He is with us.

⎧ Break the bread; taste the wine:
⎨ Know his grace; find his peace:
⎩ We'll pro-claim till he comes

1 — Christ is with us here.
2, 3 — *Refrain*

Feast on Je - sus here. In this bread
Je - sus cru - ci - fied.

there is heal - ing; in this cup there's life for - ev - er.

In this mo - ment by the Spir - it Christ is with us here.

WORDS: Graham Kendrick
MUSIC: Graham Kendrick

HERE IS BREAD
68.65 with Refrain

© 1992 Make Way Music, admin. by Music Services, Inc.

2267 Taste and See

Taste and see, taste and see the good - ness

of the Lord. _____ O taste and see, taste and

Stanzas included in other editions.

WORDS: James E. Moore (Ps. 34:8)
MUSIC: James E. Moore

TASTE AND SEE
Irregular with Refrain

© 1983 GIA Publications, Inc.

As We Gather at Your Table   2268

1. As we gath - er at your ta - ble, as we
2. Turn our wor - ship in - to wit - ness in the
3. Gra - cious Spir - it, help us sum - mon oth - er

lis - ten to your word, help us know, O God, your
sac - ra - ment of life; send us forth to love and
guests to share that feast where tri - um - phant Love will

pres - ence; let our hearts and minds be
serve you, bring - ing peace where there is
wel - come those who had been last and

stirred. Nour-ish us with sa - cred sto - ry till we
strife. Give us, Christ, your great com - pas - sion to for -
least. There no more will en - vy blind us nor will

claim it as our own; teach us through this ho - ly
give as you for - gave; may we still be - hold your
pride our peace de - stroy, as we join with saints and

ban - quet how to make Love's vic - tory known.
im - age in the world you died to save.
an - gels to re - peat the sound - ing joy.

WORDS: Carl P. Daw, Jr.
MUSIC: Skinner Chávez-Melo

RAQUEL
87.87 D

2269   Come, Share the Lord

1. We gath-er here in Je-sus' name, his love is
(3. He joins us) here, he breaks the bread, the Lord who
(5. We'll gath-er) soon where an-gels sing; we'll see the

burn-ing in our hearts like liv-ing flame; for through the
pours the cup is ris-en from the dead; the one we
glo-ry of our Lord and com-ing King; now we an-

lov-ing Son the Fa-ther makes us one: ⎱
love the most is now our gra-cious host: ⎬ Come, take the
ti-ci-pate the feast for which we wait: ⎰

Fine

bread; come, drink the wine; come, share the Lord.

2. No one is a stran-ger here, — ev-ery-one be-
4. We are now a fam-i-ly of which the Lord is

longs; find-ing our for-give-ness here, we in
head; though un-seen he meets us here in the

turn for-give all wrongs. 3. He joins us
break-ing of the bread. 5. We'll gath-er

WORDS: Bryan Jeffery Leech   DIVERNON
MUSIC: Bryan Jeffery Leech   Irregular
© 1984, 1987 Fred Bock Music Co.

EUCHARIST (HOLY COMMUNION, LORD'S SUPPER), *see further:*

2126   All Who Hunger

He Has Made Me Glad

2270

I will en-ter his gates with thanks-giv-ing in my heart, I will

en - ter his courts with praise. I will

say, "This is the day that the Lord has made." I

will re - joice, for he has made me glad.

Refrain

He has made me glad, he has made me glad. I

will re - joice, for he has made me glad.

He has made me glad, he has made me glad. I

will re - joice, for he has made me glad.

WORDS: Leona Von Brethorst (Ps. 100:2, 4; 118:24)
MUSIC: Leona Von Brethorst

LEONA
Irregular with Refrain

2271 Come! Come! Everybody Worship
(Vengan Todos Adoremos)

Refrain

Come! Come! Ev-ery-bod-y wor-ship with a prayer or song of praise!
¡Ven - gan to - dos a - do - re - mos con can - tos y o - ra - ción!

Fine

Come! Come! Ev-ery-bod-y wor-ship! Wor-ship God al - ways!
¡Ven - gan to - dos a - do - re - mos a nues - tro Se - ñor!

1. Wor-ship and re - mem-ber to keep the Sab-bath day.
2. Wor-ship and re - mem-ber the Lord's un - end - ing care,
3. Wor-ship and re - mem-ber your bless-ings great and small.
4. Wor-ship and re - mem-ber how Je - sus long a - go
5. Wor-ship and re - mem-ber that God is like a light,

D.C.

Take a rest and think of God; put your work a - way!
reach-ing out to love and help peo - ple ev - ery - where!
Give to God an of - fer - ing; show your thanks for all!
taught us how to talk to God; some-thing we should know!
show-ing you the way to go; ev - er burn - ing bright!

WORDS: Natalie Sleeth; Spanish trans. by Mary Lou Santillán-Baert
MUSIC: Natalie Sleeth

NATALIE
66.75 with Refrain

2272 Holy Ground

We are stand - ing _____ on ho - ly ground, _____

_____ and I know that there are an - gels all a -

WORDS: Geron Davis (Exod. 3:5)
MUSIC: Geron Davis

HOLY GROUND
Irregular

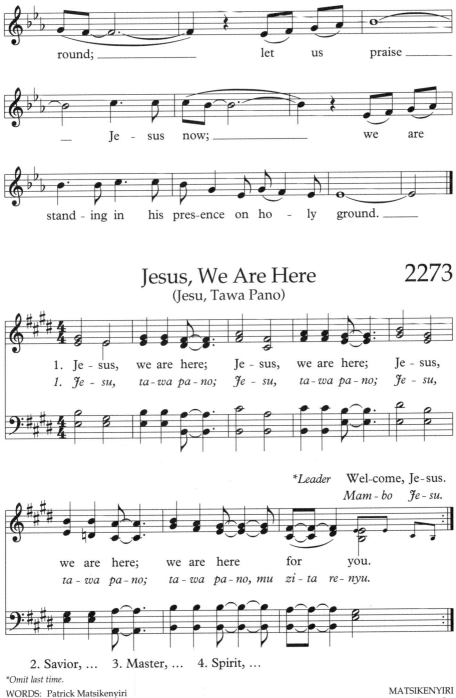

round; _____ let us praise _____

Je - sus now; _____ we are

stand - ing in his pres-ence on ho - ly ground. _____

Jesus, We Are Here
(Jesu, Tawa Pano)

2273

1. Je - sus, we are here; Je - sus, we are here; Je - sus,
1. *Je - su,   ta-wa pa - no;   Je - su,   ta-wa pa - no;   Je - su,*

Leader Wel-come, Je-sus.
Mam - bo   Je - su.

we are here; we are here for you.
ta - wa pa - no;   ta - wa pa - no, mu zi - ta re - nyu.

2. Savior, ...   3. Master, ...   4. Spirit, ...

Omit last time.

WORDS: Patrick Matsikenyiri
MUSIC: Patrick Matsikenyiri

MATSIKENYIRI
Irregular

2274

Come, All You People
(Uyai Mose)

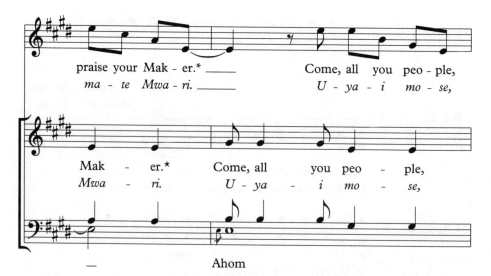

Other words may be substituted such as "Savior," "Spirit," and so forth.

WORDS: Alexander Gondo
MUSIC: Alexander Gondo; arr. by John Bell

UYAI MOSE
Irregular

2275

Kyrie

WORDS: Ancient Greek
MUSIC: Based on Mvt. II from *Symphony No. 9* by Antonín Dvořák;
    arr. by Ruth Elaine Schram

NEW WORLD
Irregular

Arr. © 1998 Alfred Publishing Co.

Glory to God in the Highest

2276

Glo-ry to God in the high - est! Sing glo-ry to God! _____ Glo-ry to God in the high - est, and peace to God's peo-ple on earth! _____

Stanzas included in other editions.

WORDS: From the liturgy (Luke 2:14)
MUSIC: David Haas (from *Mass of Light*)

GLORIA (HAAS)
Irregular

© 1988 GIA Publications, Inc.

Lord, Have Mercy

2277

Lord, have mer - cy. Christ, have mer - cy.

Fine

Lord, have mer - cy on us. _____

Though red like crim-son is my sin, _____ great - er

D.C. al Fine

yet is for - give - ness found in Christ. _____

WORDS: Swee Hong Lim (Isa. 1:18)
MUSIC: Swee Hong Lim

SINGAPURA
Irregular

© 1995 General Board of Global Ministries, GBGMusik

2278 The Lord's Prayer

WORDS: Matt. 6:9-13
MUSIC: Anon.; arr. by Al Oppenheimer

LORD'S PRAYER (OPPENHEIMER)
Irregular

2279 The Trees of the Field

You shall go out with joy __ and be led forth with peace; _ the
moun-tains and the hills will break forth be-fore you; there'll be
shouts of joy, _ and all the trees of the field will clap, will clap their
hands. And all the trees of the field will clap their hands, __ the
trees of the field will clap their hands, __ the trees of the
field will clap their hands _ while you go out with joy.

*Clap hands.

WORDS: Steffi Geiser Ruben (Isa. 55:12)

MUSIC: Stuart Dauermann

© 1975 Lillenas Publishing Co., admin. by The Copyright Co.

THE TREES OF THE FIELD
Irregular

2280 The Lord Bless and Keep You

The Lord bless and keep you, the Lord make his
(The) Lord bless and keep you, the Lord lift his

WORDS: Jim Strathdee (Num. 6:24-26)

MUSIC: Jim Strathdee

© 1981 Desert Flower Music

STRATHDEE BENEDICTION
Irregular

face to shine on you and be gra - cious, gra
coun - te - nance on you and give peace, _____ give you

1 2

cious. The
peace. Sha - lom. _____ Sha - lom. _____
(_ A - men.) _____

May You Run and Not Be Weary 2281

May you run and not be wea - ry. May your

heart be filled with song. __ And may the

love of God con - tin - ue to give you hope and

keep you strong. And may you run and not be wea -

ry. May your life be filled with joy! __ And may the

road you trav - el al-ways lead you home. _

WORDS: Paul Murakami and Handt Hanson (Isa. 40:31)
MUSIC: Paul Murakami and Handt Hanson
© 1991 Changing Church Forum

PRINCE OF PEACE
Irregular

2282

I'll Fly Away

1. Some glad morn-ing when this life is o'er, I'll fly a-
2. When the shad-ows of this life have gone, fly a-way,
3. Just a few more wea-ry days and then,

way; fly a-way;

to a home on God's ce-les-tial shore,
like a bird from pris-on bars has flown,
to a land where joys shall nev-er end,

Refrain

I'll fly a-way. I'll fly a-way, O glo-ry,
fly a-way, fly a-way. fly a-way,

I'll fly a-way. When I die, hal-le-
fly a-way, in the morn-ing.

WORDS: Albert E. Brumley (Isa. 55:6; 2 Cor. 5:8)
MUSIC: Albert E. Brumley

I'LL FLY AWAY
94.94 with Refrain

lu - jah, by and by, I'll fly a - way.
fly a - way, fly a - way.

For All the Saints

2283

1. For all the saints who've shown your
2. For all the saints who loved your
3. For all the saints who named your
4. Bless all whose will or name or

love in how they live and where they
name, whose faith in - creased the Sav - ior's
will, and showed the king - dom com - ing
love re - flects the grace of heaven a -

move, for mind - ful wo - men, car - ing
fame, who sang your songs and shared your
still through self - less pro - test, prayer, and
bove. Though un - ac - claimed by earth - ly

men, ac - cept our gra - ti - tude a - gain.
word, ac - cept our gra - ti - tude, good Lord.
praise, ac - cept the gra - ti - tude we raise.
powers, your life through theirs has hal - lowed ours.

WORDS: John Bell
MUSIC: English folk melody
O WALY WALY
LM
Words © 1996 WGRG The Iona Community (Scotland), admin. by GIA Publications, Inc.

2284   Joy in the Morning

1. There'll be joy in the morn-ing on that day,
2. There'll be peace and con-tent-ment ev - er - more,
3. There'll be love and for - give-ness ev - ery - where,

there'll be joy in the morn-ing on that day,
there'll be peace and con - tent-ment ev - er - more,
there'll be love and for - give-ness ev - ery - where,

for the day - light will dawn when the dark - ness is gone,
ev - ery heart, ev - ery voice on that day will re - joice,
and the way of the Lord will that day be re - stored,

there'll be joy in the morn-ing on that day.
there'll be peace and con - tent-ment ev - er - more.
there'll be love and for - give-ness ev - ery - where.

WORDS: Natalie Sleeth (Ps. 30:5)
MUSIC: Natalie Sleeth

JOY IN THE MORNING
Irregular

© 1977 Hope Publishing Co.

ACKNOWLEDGMENTS

Use of copyrighted material is gratefully acknowledged by the publisher. Every effort has been made to locate the administrator of each copyright. The publisher would be pleased to have any errors or omissions brought to its attention. All copyright notices include the following declarations: All rights reserved. International copyright secured. Used with permission.

Abingdon Press (see The Copyright Company)

Above the Rim Music (ASCAP) (see BMG Songs, Inc.)

Acuff-Rose Music Publishing, Inc.; 65 Music Square, West; Nashville, TN 37203; (615) 321-5000; FAX 327-0560

Doris Akers (see Hal Leonard Corporation)

Albert E. Brumley & Sons (SESAC) (see Integrated Copyright Group). "I'll Fly Away" in *Wonderful Message* by Hartford Music Co.

Alfred Publishing Co., Inc.; 16320 Roscoe Blvd.; Van Nuys, CA 91410-0003; (818) 891-5999

Anglican Church of Canada; 600 Jarvis St.; Toronto, ON M4Y 2J6 (416) 924-9199x277; FAX (416) 924-0211; glight@national.anglican.ca

Ariose Music (ASCAP) (see EMI Christian Music Group)

Augsburg Fortress Publishers; P.O. Box 1209; Minneapolis, MN 55440-1209; (612) 330-3300

Birdwing Music (ASCAP) (see EMI Christian Music Group)

BMG Songs (ASCAP) (see EMI Christian Music Group)

BMG Songs, Inc. (ASCAP) 1400 18th Ave., S.; Nashville, TN 37212; (615) 858-1300

Boosey & Co., Ltd. (see Boosey & Hawkes, Inc.)

Boosey & Hawkes, Inc.; 24 East 21st St.; New York, NY 10010

Brentwood-Benson Music Publishing, Inc. (ASCAP); Attn: Copyright Administration; 741 Cool Springs Blvd.; Franklin, TN 37067

Brier Patch Music; 4324 Canal Southwest; Grandville, MI 49418; (616) 534-1113 (FAX)

Broadman Press (see Van Ness Press, Inc.)

Bud John Songs, Inc. (ASCAP) (see EMI Christian Music Group)

Carol Joy Music (ASCAP) (see Integrated Copyright Group)

Celebration (see The Copyright Company)

Chalice Press; Christian Board of Publication; 1316 Convention Plaza; Box 179; St. Louis, MO 63166-0179; (800) 366-3383; FAX (314) 231-2027; curriculum@cbp21.com

Changing Church Forum; 200 E. Nicollet Blvd.; Burnsville, MN 55337; (800) 874-2044; FAX (612) 435-8015

Skinner Chávez-Melo; c/o Juan Francisco Chávez-Melo; Juarez no. 85 Casa 19; Col. Ampliacion Miguel Hidalgo; Tlalpan 14250; Mexico D. F. Mexico; (011) 525-528-1884; chavezme@prodigy.net.mx

Susan Palo Cherwien (see Augsburg Fortress Publishers)

Choristers Guild; 2834 W. Kingsley Rd.; Garland, TX 75041-2498; (972) 271-1521; FAX (972) 840-3113

Church Publishing, Inc.; 445 Fifth Ave.; New York, NY 10016; (212) 592-1800x360; FAX (212) 779-3392

J. Jefferson Cleveland (see William B. McClain)

Cokesbury (see The Copyright Company)

Common Cup Co.; 7591 Gray Ave.; Burnby BC V5J 3ZY; (604) 434-8323

Concionero Abierto; c/o Pablo Sosa; Eparlaco 634; 1406 Buenos Aires, Argentina

Concordia Publishing House; 3558 South Jefferson Ave; St. Louis, MO 63118-3968; (314) 268-1000; FAX (314) 268-1329; www.cph.org

Damean Music (see GIA Publications, Inc.)

Dayspring Music, Inc. (BMI) (see Acuff-Rose Music Publishing, Inc.)

Desert Flower Music; P.O. Box 1476; Carmichael, CA 95609; (916) 481-2999

Andrew Donaldson; 14 Hambly Ave.; Toronto, Ontario M4E 2R6; (416) 691-1158; FAX: (416) 690-9967; seraph@pathcom.com

Doubleday; 1540 Broadway; New York, NY 10036; (212) 782-8957; FAX (212) 782-8898

Dr. Margaret P. Douroux; Rev. Earl Pleasant Publishing; P.O. Box 3247; Thousand Oaks, CA 91359; (818) 991-3728; FAX (818) 991-2567; GospelMeg@aol.com

Delores Dufner (see OCP Publications)

Earthsongs; 220 NW 29th St.; Corallis, OR 97330

E.C. Schirmer; 138 Ipswich St.; Boston, MA 02215

EMI Christian Music Group; P.O. Box 5085; 101 Winners Circle; Brentwood, TN 37024-5085; (615) 371-4300

Ever Devoted Music (see The Copyright Company)

Stanley M. Farr; 518 Fairmont Rd.; Morgantown, WV 26505

F.E.L. Publications (see The Lorenz Corporation)

Fred Bock Music Co., Inc.; 18345 Ventura Blvd., Suite 212; Tarzana, CA 91356; (818) 996-6181; FAX (618) 996-2043

Gaither Copyright Management; P.O. Box 737; Alexandria, IN 46001; (765) 724-8233; FAX (765) 724-8290

Gamut Music Productions; 704 Saddle Trail Ct.; Hermitage, TN 37076

Steve Garnaas-Holmes; 20 Greenbrier Dr.; Missoula, MT 59802

General Board of Global Ministries, GBGMusik; 475 Riverside Dr.; Room 350; New York, NY 10115 (print licenses 2109 and 2095)

GIA Publications, Inc.; 7404 S. Mason Ave.; Chicago, IL 60638; (800) GIA-1358; FAX (708) 496-3828

Hal Leonard Corp.; 777 W. Bluemound Rd.; Milwaukee, WI 53213

Marilyn Houser Hamm; Box 1887; Altona, Manitoba; Canada R0G 0B0; FAX (204) 831-5675

Harold Flammer, Inc.; 49 Waring Dr.; Delaware Water Gap, PA 18327-0690; FAX (717) 476-5247

Harper Collins Religious (see The Copyright Company)

Carl Haywood; 5228 Foxboro Landing; Virginia Beach, VA 23464 (757) 467-8971; FAX (757) 467-2172

Heart of the City Music; 300 E. Main St.; Anoka, MN 55503; (612) 323-4361

Hillsongs Publishing (ASCAP) (see Integrity's Hosanna! Music)

Hinshaw Music, Inc.; P.O. Box 470; Chapel Hill, NC 27514-0470; (919) 933-1691; FAX (919) 967-3399

Hodder and Stoughton Limited; 338 Euston Rd.; London, NW1 3BH; England; FAX 020-787-36308

Hope Publishing Company; 380 S. Main Pl.; Carol Stream, IL 60188; (800) 323-1049; FAX (630) 665-2552; www.hopepublishing.com

House of Mercy Music (see The Copyright Company)

Jane Parker Huber (see Westminster John Knox Press)

Coni Huisman; 3239 Tettis Ave., NE; Ada, MI 49301

Integrated Copyright Group; P.O. Box 24149; Nashville, TN 37202

Integrity Music, Inc.; 1000 Cody Rd.; Mobile, AL 36695-3425; (334) 633-9000; FAX (334) 633-9998

Integrity's Hosanna! Music (ASCAP); c/o Integrity Music, Inc.; 1000 Cody Rd.; Mobile, AL 36695-3425; (334) 633-9000; FAX (334) 633-9998

John T. Benson Publishing Co. (ASCAP) (see Brentwood-Benson Music Publishing, Inc.)

Jonathan Mark Music (ASCAP) (see EMI Christian Music Group)

Jubilate Hymns (see Hope Publishing Company)

Juniper Landing Music (see Word Music)

Kingsway's Thank You Music (see EMI Christian Music Group)

ACKNOWLEDGMENTS

Ron Klusmeier; 345 Pym St.; Parksville, B.C., Canada V9P 1C8; (250) 954-2319; FAX (250) 954-1683; staff@musiklus.com

Latter Rain Music (ASCAP) (see EMI Christian Music Group)

Geonyong Lee; c/o St. Paul Church; 2-20-1 Megura, Gohonggi; Tokyo, Japan 153-0053; FAX 82-2-520-8109

Les Presses de Taizé (see GIA Publications, Inc.)

Lillenas Publishing Company (see The Copyright Company)

Lilly Mack Music (BMI); 421 E. Beach; Inglewood, CA 90302; (310) 677-5603; FAX (310) 677-0250

Lutheran Book of Worship (see Augsburg Fortress Publishers)

Lynn C. Franklin Associates, Ltd.; 1350 Broadway, Suite 2015; New York, NY 10018; (212) 868-6311; FAX (212) 868-6312; lcf@fsainc.com

William B. McClain; c/o The Estate of J. Jefferson Cleveland; 4500 Massachusetts Ave., NW; Washington, D.C. 20016

Make Way Music (see Music Services, Inc.)

James K. Manley; Music by Jim Manley; 690 Persian Dr., #67; Sunnyvale, CA 94089; (408) 747-0667; jmanley@aol.com

Maranatha! Music (see The Copyright Company)

Maranatha Praise, Inc. (see The Copyright Company)

Martin and Morris (see Hal Leonard Corporation)

Matters Most Music (ASCAP) (see Brentwood-Benson Music Publishing, Inc.)

Meadowgreen Music Company (ASCAP) (see EMI Christian Music Group)

Mercy/Vineyard Publishing (see Music Services, Inc.)

Mole Hill Music (see Brentwood-Benson Music Publishing, Inc.)

Mountain Spring Music (ASCAP) (see EMI Christian Music Group)

Music Services, Inc. (ASCAP); 209 Chapelwood Dr.; Franklin, TN 37069; (615) 794-9015; FAX (615) 794-0793; www.musicservices.org

New Song Creations; R.R. 1, Box 454; Erin, TN 37061

New Spring Publishing, Inc. (ASCAP) (see Brentwood-Benson Music Publishing, Inc.)

Fintan O'Carroll (see OCP Publications)

OCP Publications; Attn: Licensing Dept.; P.O. Box 18030; Portland, OR 97218-0030; (800) 548-8749; FAX (503) 282-3486; liturgy@ocp.org ("Make Me a Channel of Your Peace" is dedicated to Mrs. Frances Tracy)

Oxford University Press; Great Clarendon St.; Oxford OX2 6DP, UK; 441-865-267254; FAX 441-865-267749

Oxford University Press, Inc.; 198 Madison Ave.; New York, NY 10016-4314; (212) 726-6000; FAX (212) 726-6444

Pamela Kay Music (ASCAP) (see EMI Christian Music Group)

Pilot Point Music (see The Copyright Company)

Prism Tree Music (see The Lorenz Corporation)

John S. Rice; Estate of John S. Rice; c/o Brian H. Davidson, Executor; 10619 Alameda Dr.; Knoxville, TN 37392-2502

River Oaks Music Company (BMI) (see EMI Christian Music Group)

ROM Administration; P.O. Box 1252; Fairhope, AL 36533; (334) 929-2411; FAX (334) 929-2404

Julian B. Rush; 1433 Williams St.; Unit 302; Denver, CO 80218-2531; (303) 837-0166x101; FAX (303) 837-9213

Taihei Sato; 9-2-20-1402 Takashimadaira; Habushi-ku; Tokyo 175; Japan

Scripture in Song (ASCAP) (see Integrity Music, Inc.)

Selah Publishing Co. Inc.; 58 Pearl St.; Kingston, NY 12402; (914) 338-2816; FAX (914) 338-2991; www.selahpub.com

Shepherd's Fold Music (BMI) (see EMI Christian Music Group)

Singspiration Music (ASCAP) (see Brentwood-Benson Music Publishing, Inc.)

Songchannel Music Co. (ASCAP) (see EMI Christian Music Group)

SongWard Music (see Brentwood-Benson Music Publishing, Inc.)

Sound III, Inc. (see Universal-MCA Music Publishing)

Sovereign Music UK; P.O. Box 356; Leighton Buzzard, Beds. LU7 8WP UK; 44-1-525-385578; FAX 44-1-525-372743; SovereignM@aol.com

Leo Sowerby; Ronald Stalford, Executor; Estate of Leo Sowerby; 136 Coolidge Rd.; Worcester, MA 01602

Stainer & Bell Ltd. (see Hope Publishing Co.)

Linda Stassen (see New Song Creations)

Straightway Music (ASCAP) (see EMI Christian Music Group)

The American Lutheran Church (see Augsburg Fortress Publishers)

The Church Pension Fund (see Church Publishing, Inc.)

The Copyright Company; 40 Music Square, East; Nashville, TN 37203; FAX (615) 244-5591

The Hymn Society (see Hope Publishing Company)

The Kruger Organization, Inc.; 4501 Connecticut Ave., NW; Suite 711; Washington, DC 20008; (202) 966-3280; FAX (202) 364-1367

The Lorenz Corporation; 501 East Third St.; Dayton, OH 45402-2118; (937) 228-6118; FAX (937) 223-2042; info@Lorenz.com

The Pilgrim Press; 700 Prospect Ave., E.; Cleveland, OH 44115

The United Methodist Publishing House (see The Copyright Company)

John D. Thornburg; 1211 Preston Rd.; Dallas, TX 75230; (214) 363-2479; FAX (214) 373-3972

ThreeFold Amen Music (see ROM Administration)

Desmond Tutu (see Lynn C. Franklin Associates, Ltd.)

Unichappell Music, Inc. (see Hal Leonard Corporation)

Universal-MCA Music Publishing (see Warner Bros. Publications U.S., Inc.)

Universal-PolyGram International Publishing, Inc. (see Warner Bros. Publications U.S., Inc.)

Utryck (see Walton Music Corporation)

Utterbach Music, Inc. (see Warner Bros. Publications U.S., Inc.)

Van Ness Press, Inc.; FAX (615) 251-2869

Christopher Walker (see OCP Publications)

Mary Lu Walker; 16 Brown Rd.; Corning, NY 14830; (607) 936-4801; marluwalk@aol.com

William L. Wallace; 215A Mt. Pleasant Rd.; Christchurch, New Zealand; FAX +64 3 3840111

Walton Music Corporation; P.O. Box 167; Bynum, NC 27228; (919) 542-5548; FAX (919) 542-5527; writeus@waltonmusic.com

Warner Bros. Publications U.S., Inc.; 15800 Northwest 48th Ave.; Miami, FL 33014

Westminster John Knox Press; 100 Witherspoon St.; Louisville, KY 40202-1396; (502) 569-5342; FAX (502) 569-5113 ("Wonder of Wonders" is from A Singing Faith)

WGRG (See GIA Publications, Inc.)

Wendell Whalum; The Estate of Wendell Whalum; c/o Clarie Whalum; 2439 Greenwood Cir.; East Point, GA 30344

Whole Armor/Full Armor Music (see The Kruger Organization, Inc.)

Willing Heart Music (see The Copyright Company)

Word Music (see Acuff-Rose Music Publishing, Inc.)

Word Music, Inc. (see Acuff-Rose Music Publishing, Inc.)

John Ylvisaker; Box 321; Waverly, IA 50677

Darlene Zschech (ASCAP) (see Integrity's Hosanna! Music)

INDEX OF FIRST LINES AND COMMON TITLES